WORD
MEANINGS
in the
New Testament

6

WORD
MEANINGS
in the
New Testament

volume 6

HEBREWS—REVELATION

by

Ralph Earle, Th.D.

BBH

BAKER BOOK HOUSE
Grand Rapids, Michigan 49506

ISBN: 0-8010-3421-3

Permission to quote from the following copyrighted versions of the Bible is acknowledged with appreciation:

The *New American Standard Bible* (NASB), © The Lockman Foundation, 1960, 1962, 1963, 1968, 1971, 1972, 1973, 1975, 1977.

The Holy Bible, New International Version (NIV), copyright © 1978 by the New York International Bible Society.

The *Revised Standard Version of the Bible* (RSV), copyrighted 1946, 1952, © 1971, 1973.

Contents

Preface

It is with sincere gratitude to God that we come to the completion of the six volumes of *Word Meanings in the New Testament.* The first volume to be published (vol. 3) appeared in 1974. Across more than a dozen years the total project has engaged our attention, interspersed with a heavy schedule of preaching, teaching, translating (NIV), and the writing of a dozen other books *(Peloubet's Notes).* We thank God for health and strength to complete this task.

The heading of each discussion consists of a word or phrase from the King James Version. The original Greek is then presented and interpreted.

It is our prayer that each reader will find help in understanding and expounding the inspired New Testament.

February 1984   —RALPH EARLE

Abbreviations and Sources

AG	W. F. Arndt and F. W. Gingrich. *A Greek-English Lexicon of the New Testament.* 2nd ed. Chicago: University of Chicago Press, 1979.
Am. Heritage Dict.	*American Heritage Dictionary*
A-S	G. Abbott-Smith. *A Manual Greek Lexicon of the New Testament.* 2nd ed. Edinburgh: T. & T. Clark, 1923.
Bengel	John Albert Bengel. *Gnomon of the New Testament.* 5 vols. Edinburgh: T. & T. Clark, 1860.
Bruce	F. F. Bruce. *Epistle to the Hebrews,* in *New International Commentary on the New Testament.* Grand Rapids: Wm. B. Eerdmans Publishing Co., 1964.
BS	Adolf Deissmann. *Bible Studies.* Edinburgh: T. & T. Clark, 1901.
Cremer	Hermann Cremer. *Biblico-Theological Lexicon of New Testament Greek.* Trans. W. Urwick. Edinburgh: T. & T. Clark, 1878.
EGT	*Expositor's Greek Testament.* 5 vols. Grand Rapids: Wm. B. Eerdmans Publishing Co., n.d.
ICC	*International Critical Commentary*
Ladd	George E. Ladd. *A Commentary on the Revelation of John.* Grand Rapids: Wm. B. Eerdmans Publishing Co., 1972.
LAE	Adolf Deissmann. *Light from the Ancient East.* New York: George H. Doran Co., 1927.
Lange	John Peter Lange. *Commentary on the Holy Scriptures.* Grand Rapids: Zondervan Publishing House, n.d.
Liddell-Scott	H. G. Liddell and Robert Scott. *A Greek-English Lexicon.* Rev. by H. S. Jones. 9th ed. Oxford: Clarendon Press, 1940.

Mayor	Joseph B. Mayor. *Epistle of St. James.* 1913; reprint. Grand Rapids: Zondervan Publishing House, 1954.
McDowell	Edward McDowell. *The Meaning and Message of the Book of Revelation.* Nashville: Broadman Press, 1951.
Mounce	Robert H. Mounce. *The Book of Revelation,* in *New International Commentary on the New Testament.* Grand Rapids: Wm. B. Eerdmans Publishing Co., 1977.
NASB	*New American Standard Bible*
NIV	*The Holy Bible, New International Version*
RSV	*Revised Standard Version of the Bible*
Swete	Henry Barclay Swete. *The Apocalypse of St. John.* 1909; reprint. Grand Rapids: Wm. B. Eerdmans Publishing Co., 1951.
TDNT	*Theological Dictionary of the New Testament.* Edited by G. Kittel and G. Friedrich. Trans. by G. W. Bromiley. 10 vols. Grand Rapids: Wm. B. Eerdmans Publishing Co., 1964-76.
Trench	R. C. Trench. *Synonyms of the New Testament.* 9th ed. 1880; reprint. Grand Rapids: Wm. B. Eerdmans Publishing Co., 1947.
VGT	J. H. Moulton and George Milligan. *The Vocabulary of the Greek Testament.* Grand Rapids: Wm. B. Eerdmans Publishing Co., 1949.
Westcott	B. F. Westcott. *Epistle to the Hebrews.* London: Macmillan, 1892.
WM	Ralph Earle. *Word Meanings in the New Testament.* 6 vols. Kansas City: Beacon Hill Press of Kansas City, 1974-84.
WP	A. T. Robertson. *Word Pictures in the New Testament.* 6 vols. New York: Richard R. Smith, 1930-33.
WS	Marvin Vincent. *Word Studies in the New Testament.* 4 vols. 1887; reprint. Grand Rapids: Wm. B. Eerdmans Publishing Co., 1946.

HEBREWS

❧◎◍◎☙

At Sundry Times and in Divers Manners (1:1)

The first three words of this Epistle are *polymerōs kai polytropōs. Kai,* of course, means "and." That leaves us the two adverbs to look at.

"At sundry times" is one word in Greek, *polymerōs* (only here in NT). *Poly* means "many" (cf. English use as a prefix); *merōs* means "part." So the adverb literally means "in many parts," or "in many portions" (NASB). "In divers manners" is *polytropōs. Tropōs* means "way"—so, "in many ways" (NASB).

Marcus Dods gives an excellent treatment of these two adverbs. He writes:

> *Polymerōs* points to the fragmentary character of former revelations. They were given piece-meal, bit by bit, part by part, as the people needed and were able to receive them. The revelation of God was essentially progressive; all was not disclosed at once, because all could not at once be understood *(EGT, 4:247).*

Dods goes on to say:

> His speaking was also *polytropōs* . . . not in one stereotyped manner but in modes varying with the message, the messenger, and those to whom the word is sent.

Sometimes, therefore, God spoke by an institution [for instance, the Tabernacle and its offerings], sometimes by parable, sometimes in a psalm, sometimes in an act of righteous indignation. . . . These features of previous revelations, so prominently set and expressed so grandiloquently, cannot have been meant to disparage them, rather to bring into view their affluence and pliability and many-sided application to the growing receptivity and varying needs of men *(4:248)*.

By His Son (1:2)

The Greek reads *en whiō*—literally, "in a son." This emphasizes the character of the new revelation in Christ; it was a *personal* revelation. The previous revelations had been in prophecies, types, and symbols. But an impersonal revelation of a person must always be an imperfect one. So at last God sent His Son. Only a personal revelation of a person can be a perfect revelation. Christ is the perfect Revelation of God.

The Worlds (1:2)

The Greek says *tous aiōnas*—literally, "the ages." B. F. Westcott makes this helpful comment: "The universe may be regarded either in its actual constitution as a whole *(ho cosmos),* or as an order which exists through time developed in successive stages. There are obvious reasons why the latter mode of representation should be adopted here" (p. 8).

Brightness (1:3)

The Greek word *apaugasma* (only here in NT) is used passively in the sense of "reflection" (cf. RSV). But the active meaning, "effulgence" or "radiance" (NASB, NIV), is that adopted by the bulk of the Early Church fathers and so is to be preferred here (Kittel, TDNT, 1:508).

Express Image (1:3)

This is one word in Greek, *charactēr* (only here in NT). It first meant "a tool for engraving," and then "a stamp or impress," as on a coin or seal (A-S, 479). It is that by which a person or thing can be recognized (cf. our use of *character*). Probably the best translation, suggested by Arndt and Gingrich, is "exact representation" (NASB, NIV).

Person (1:3)

The Greek word *hypostasis* has been taken over into English as a technical theological term. It literally means "that which stands under," as a support or foundation. Then it came to mean "reality . . . that in virtue of which a thing is what it is, the essence of any being." Westcott goes on to say that Christ "is the expression of the 'essence' of God. He brings the Divine before us at once perfectly and definitely according to the measure of our powers" (p. 13). Marcus Dods suggests: "To the English ear, perhaps, 'nature' or 'essence' better conveys the meaning" (EGT, 4:251). So we can use "nature" (NASB) or "being" (NIV). Koester suggests that in the Septuagint *hypostasis* is the "underlying reality behind something" (TDNT, 8:582).

Spirits (1:7)

This is the plural of the noun *pneuma*, which occurs 385 times in the NT. In over 200 of those times it refers to the Holy Spirit. Only once in the KJV is it translated "wind" (John 3:8). Yet that is the rendering here in the RSV, NASB, and NIV. The reason is the parallel with "flames of fire" in the next line of poetry (see NIV). Westcott says, *"winds,* not *spirits.* The context imperatively requires this rendering" (p. 25).

Fellows (1:9)

This is the plural of the adjective *metochos,* which literally means "sharing in" or "partaking of." Used as a substantive here, it means "partners" or "associates," and so "companions" (NASB, NIV).

Let Them Slip (2:1)

The verb (only here in NT) is *pararreō* (in the second aorist pass. subj.), which means "drift away" (NASB, NIV), as all good commentators and versions agree. The KJV rendering is based on the early use of the verb (as in Plutarch) for a ring slipping away from a finger. It was also used in the sense of "be careless, neglect" (Liddell-Scott, 1322). B. F. Westcott comments:

> The idea is not that of simple forgetfulness, but of being swept along past the sure anchorage which is within reach. . . . We are all continuously exposed to the action of currents of opinion, habit, action, which tend to carry us away insensibly from the position which we ought to maintain *(p. 37).*

Recompence of Reward (2:2)

This is one word in the Greek: *misthapodosia,* which is found only in Hebrews (here; 10:35; 11:26). It literally means "payment of wages." In the other two passages it means "reward." But here, as Arndt and Gingrich note, it has the unfavorable sense of "punishment" (NIV).

And Didst Set . . . Thy Hands (2:7)

This clause is not in our oldest Greek manuscript, Papyrus 46 (about A.D. 200), or in the great fourth-century manuscript, B (Vaticanus), as well as a number of later manuscripts (cf. NIV).

Captain (2:10)

The Greek word is *archēgos,* which comes from *archē,* "beginning." So it properly means "originator," "founder," or "author" (NASB, NIV). By His death, resurrection, and ascension, Jesus Christ originated our salvation. Moulton and Milligan show that the sense of "author" or "source" is strong in the papyri (VGT, 81).

Church (2:12)

The Greek word is *ecclēsia,* which is used mostly in the NT for the Christian Church. But it is also used for a Greek "assembly" (Acts 19:32, 39, 41) and is so translated (KJV, NASB, NIV, etc.). Here we find it in a quotation from the Septuagint, which constantly uses it for the congregation of Israel. So the proper translation here is "congregation" (NASB, NIV).

Him the Nature Of (2:16)

It will be noted that in the KJV these words are in italics, which means that they are not in the original. The Greek simply has: "For surely it is not angels he helps" (NIV; cf. NASB).

Make Reconciliation (2:17)

The verb is *hilaskomai.* It occurs only here and in Luke 18:13, where it is translated "be merciful"—the prayer of the tax collector in the Temple: "God be merciful to me a sinner." In Hebrews it is rendered "make propitiation" (NASB) and "make atonement" (NIV).

The exact form here is *hilaskesthai* (pres. pass. infin.). Cremer says that this means "to be reconciled, to be gracious" (p. 301). He goes on to say, "In Homer always, and in later Greek in the majority of cases, *hilaskesthai* denotes a religious procedure: *to make the gods propitious, to cause them to be reconcilied*" (ibid.) But Cremer insists that "the idea lying at the foundation of heathen expiations is rejected by the Bible. The heathen believed the Deity to be naturally alienated in feeling from man" (pp. 302-3). Then he adds, "In the Bible the relation is a different one. God is not of Himself already alienated from man" (p. 303). But for righteousness' sake, "an expiation of sin is necessary (a substitutionary suffering of the punishment . . .); and, indeed, an expiation which He Himself and His love institute and give" (ibid.). In further pursuit of this thought, Cremer says, "Nothing happens to God, as is the case in the heathen view; therefore we never read in the Bible *hilaskesthai ton theon.* Rather something happens to man, who escapes the wrath to come" (ibid.).

Wescott puts it this way:

> The essential conception is that of altering that in the character of an object which necessarily excludes the action of the grace of God, so that God, being what He is, cannot (as we speak) look on it with favour. The "propitiation" acts on that which alienates God and not on God whose love is unchanged throughout *(p. 57).*

In Kittel's *Theological Dictionary of the New Testament* Buechsel says of *hilaskomai* and its compound, *exilaskomai:* "The most striking thing about the development of the terms, however, is that words which were originally used to denote man's action in relation to God cease to be used in this way in the NT and are used instead of God's action in relation to man" (3:317).

This is shown clearly by our passage here in Hebrews: It is not man but God—in the person of His Son, the "merciful and faithful high priest"—who makes reconciliation, propitiation, or atonement. This is the glorious gospel message of the NT.

For further discussion of "Propitiation" see WM, 3:80-83.

Consider (3:1)

The verb *katanoeō* is compounded of *nous,* "mind," and *kata,* which literally means "down" but in compounds also has the intensive or perfective force. So the idea is: "Put your mind down on" or "note carefully, thoroughly." Behm says that it is "closely related to *noeō,* whose literal meaning is intensified, 'to direct one's whole mind to an object'" (TDNT, 4:973), or "to consider reflectively" (p. 974). He also writes, "In Hebrews *katanoeō* is one of the verbal concepts which, used imperatively, impress upon the readers the duties involved in being a Christian: 3:1f . . . the duty of looking to the Mediator of salvation, of concentration upon His exemplary moral conduct" (p. 975). B. F. Westcott says that the verb "expresses attention and continuous observation and regard" (p. 74). So it may be translated "consider" (KJV, NASB) or, more forcefully, "fix your thoughts on" (NIV).

Profession (3:1)

The noun is *homologia.* It comes from the verb *homologeō,* which means "confess" and is so rendered 17 times in KJV, as against "profess" 3 times. The noun is used in Hebrews 3 times (cf. 4:14; 10:23) out of the 6 times it occurs in the NT (see 2 Cor. 9:13; 1 Tim. 6:12, 13). Lexicons and commentaries agree that the correct translation is "confession" (NASB; cf. NIV).

Rejoicing (3:6)

The noun is *kauchēma.* It literally means "a boast," but also "a ground or matter of glorying" (A-S, 243). Westcott comments, "The Christian hope is one of courageous exultation" (p. 78).

Provocation (3:8, 15)

Arndt and Gingrich say that the noun (not found elsewhere in NT) *parapikrasmos* means: *"embitterment,* then *revolt, rebellion* against God." They translate the phrase as "in the rebellion" (p. 621). This was adopted in the NIV.

Rest (3:11)

The noun *katapausis* is found eight times in Hebrews, twice in this chapter (vv. 11, 18), and six times in chapter 4 (vv. 1, 3 [twice], 5, 10, 11). Elsewhere it occurs only in Acts 7:49. Likewise the verb *katapauō* is found only in Acts 14:18 and three times in Hebrews 4 (vv. 4, 8, 10). It is here in Hebrews that we find the greatest emphasis on "rest" in the New Testament.

The verb is compounded of *pauō,* "cease," and *kata* (intensive or perfective). It suggests an entire cessation of nervous activity or struggle. The same is true of the noun. God has a beautiful, quiet rest for His people to enjoy.

Jesus (4:8)

It is true that the Greek does have *Iēsous,* "Jesus." But this is the Greek form of the Hebrew *Yehoshua,* "Joshua." In this place the obvious reference is to the OT "Joshua"; so that familiar name should be used. The KJV here is misleading to the casual or uninformed reader.

Rest (4:9)

Here we find a different Greek word, *sabbatismos* (only here in NT). It means "a keeping sabbath," and so "a

Sabbath-rest" (NIV; cf. NASB). The term is used for the deeper rest that the Christian should enjoy.

Westcott says that *sabbatismos* indicates "a rest which closes the manifold forms of earthy preparation and work . . . : not an isolated sabbath but a sabbath life." He adds, "The change of term from *katapausis* is significant" (p. 98).

Labour (4:11)

The KJV says, "Let us labour therefore to enter into that rest." To say the least, this is an odd combination of ideas.

The Greek verb translated "labour" is *spoudazō,* which means literally "to make haste," and so, "to be zealous or *eager, to give diligence"* (A-S, 414). It occurs 11 times in the NT and is translated "labour" only here (in KJV). A much better translation is "be diligent" (NASB) or "make every effort" (NIV).

Quick . . . Powerful (4:12)

The first Greek word is *zōn,* the present participle of the verb *zaō,* "to live, be alive." So it simply means "living" (NASB, NIV). (The KJV uses the obsolete "quick" for "alive" four times in the NT.)

The Greek for the second word is the adjective *energēs* (cf. *energetic*). It comes from *en* and *ergon,* "work," and so literally means "at work," or "active" (NASB, NIV).

Naked (4:13)

It is true that the adjective *gymnos* literally means "naked." But Abbott-Smith notes that metaphorically it is used for things "exposed" (p. 96). So a better translation is "open" (NASB) or "uncovered" (NIV).

Opened (4:13)

The Greek has *tetrachēlisemena*, the perfect passive participle of the verb *trachēlizō* (only here in NT). It is evidently used metaphorically here in the sense of "laid open" (A-S, 449) or "laid bare" (NASB, NIV).

Ordained (5:1)

Kathistēmi literally means "set down" or "bring down" (to a place). Then it came to be used most generally in the sense of "appoint." Westcott says that it is "the ordinary word for authoritative appointment to an office" (p. 118). Since "ordained" now has a technical usage, probably "appointed" (NASB, NIV) is better.

Have Compassion On (5:2)

The verb *metriopatheō* (only here in NT) means *"to hold one's passions or emotions in restraint; hence, To bear gently with, feel gently towards"* (A-S, 289). "Deal gently with" (NASB, NIV) best communicates the exact thought.

In That He Feared (5:7)

The Greek has the noun *eulabeia* (only here and 12:28). In secular Greek usage this word does commonly have the idea of fear or anxiety. But it also was used in the sense of piety, or reverent awe of God. Bultmann argues for both meanings as valid (TDNT, 2:751-54). He does say that in the Septuagint of Prov. 28:14 it means "religious awe." So we find in recent versions: "for his godly fear" (RSV); "because of His piety" (NASB); "because of his reverent submission" (NIV).

Westcott makes these comments:

> *Eulabeia* marks that careful and watchful reverence which pays regard to every circumstance in that with

which it has to deal. It may therefore degenerate into a timid and unworthy anxiety (Jos. *Antt.* vi.2, 179); but more commonly it expresses reverent and thoughtful shrinking from over boldness. . . . Here the word in its noblest sense is singularly appropriate. Prayer is heard as it is "according to God's will" (1 John v.14f.), and Christ by His *eulabeia* perfectly realized that submission which is obedience on one side and fellowship on the other *(p. 127).*

Author (5:9)

Aitios is an adjective meaning "causative of" or "responsible for" (A-S, 14-15). In the NT it is used only as a substantive (like a noun). It means "cause," or "source" (NASB, NIV).

Called (5:10)

The verb is *prosagoreuō* (only here in NT). It means "call, name, designate." The last of these three is used in the RSV, NASB, and NIV. Westcott says that the verb "expresses the formal and solemn ascription of the title [high priest] to Him to whom it belongs" (p. 130).

Hard to Be Uttered (5:11)

This is all one word in Greek, the compound adjective *dysermēneutos* (only here in NT). The prefix *dys* has the idea of "difficult." The rest of the word is based on the verb *hermēneuō,* "explain" or "interpret" (cf. *hermeneutics*). So "hard to explain" (RSV, NASB, NIV) is the correct translation here.

For the Time (5:12)

This could be taken as meaning "for the time being." But the Greek literally says, "because of the time" *(dia ton chronon).* The true meaning obviously is "by this time" (RSV, NASB, NIV)—that is, after such a long time as Christians.

The First Principles (5:12)

The Greek is *ta stoicheia tēs archēs.* The noun *stoicheion* (sing.) properly means "one of a series" *(stoichos).* Plutarch uses it for *"an elementary sound* or *letter* of the alphabet" and Aristotle for *"the elements* or *rudiments* of knowledge" (A-S, 418). That is clearly its meaning here.

Delling writes, "If letters are the basis of speech and their knowledge that of instruction, *stoicheion* can soon come to mean 'what is basic or primary' ... or the 'elementary details'" (TDNT, 7:679). He goes on to say, "The meaning in Hb. 5:12 is clearly 'first principles' with a slightly derogatory nuance: *ta stoicheia,* 'mere rudiments,' 'ABC.' The idea of first principles is strengthened, or brought to expression, by *tēs archēs*" (p. 687). The whole expression literally means the "elements of the beginning" (NASB marg.).

Strong Meat (5:12, 14)

The Greek is *stereas trophēs* (v. 12, gen. case) and *sterea trophē* (v. 14, nom. case). The adjective *stereos (-a, -on)* means "hard, firm, solid." *Trophē* comes from the verb *trephō,* "feed." So the correct translation here is "solid food" (RSV, NASB, NIV). The KJV rather constantly uses "meat" for all food, but this is not good American English and misleads the modern reader.

Of Full Age (5:14)

This is one word in Greek, the genitive plural of the adjective *teleios,* which comes from the noun *telos,* "end." So it means "having reached its end, finished, mature . . ." (A-S, 442). All are agreed that here it means "the mature" (RSV, NASB, NIV). Babies drink milk, but mature persons eat solid food.

Perfection (6:1)

The noun *teleiotēs* occurs elsewhere in the NT only in Col. 3:14, where it is translated "perfectness" (KJV). It comes from the noun *telos,* which means "end." So the basic idea is completeness.

The first part of this verse literally reads: "Therefore, having left the word of the beginning [Gk., *archēs*] of Christ." This ties in with 5:12, where the term *archēs* is used and where both NASB and NIV translate it as "elementary." The writer of Hebrews goes on to say: "Anyone who lives on milk, being still an infant . . . But solid food is for the mature" (5:13-14, NIV). Since "therefore" (6:1) ties our verse right into this, it would seem that "mature" is the best translation here. Delling writes, "In distinction from archē (Hb. 5:12; 6:1) *teleiotēs* is in Hb. the 'highest stage' of Christian teaching (6:1)" (TDNT, 8:79). So the primary emphasis of this exhortation is not on Christian character or experience but on advance in learning the higher teachings of the Christian faith.

World (6:5)

The Greek word *aiōn* should be translated "age," though the KJV renders it "world" 38 times and "age" only twice.

If (6:6)

In verses 4-6 there are five aorist participles in parallel construction. The fifth one is *parapesontas,* "and have fallen away." The NASB has the correct translation here: "and then have fallen away." The "if" is not justifiable. The Greek clearly indicates that one may become a partaker of the Holy Spirit—obviously a Christian—and yet fall away and be lost.

Seeing They Crucify (6:6)

This is one word in the Greek, *anastaurountas*—a present participle of continuous action. So the best translation is probably "while they are crucifying."

Herbs (6:7)

The Greek word (only here in NT) is *botanē* (botanay) from which we get *botany*. It means "fodder, herb, plant" (AG). So it can be translated "vegetation" (NASB).

Dressed (6:7)

The verb *geōrgeō* (only here in NT) is compounded of *gē*, "earth" or "land," and the verb *ergō* (from *ergon*, "work"). So it means "work the land" (or "ground"). Today we would say "tilled" (NASB) or "farmed" (NIV).

Immutable (6:18)

The adjective is *ametathetos*—*a*-negative plus the verb *metatithēmi*, "place across" or "change." In verse 17 it is in the neuter and used as a substantive. These are the only two occurrences of this adjective in the NT. God is unchanging and unchangeable in His purpose (cf. NASB, NIV).

Consolation (6:18)

The noun *paraclēsis* occurs 29 times in the Greek NT. In the KJV it is translated "consolation" 14 times, "exhortation" 8 times, "comfort" 6 times, and "intreaty" once.

The word that today combines these meanings is "encouragement" (NASB; cf. NIV). That fits well with "hope" here. (For further discussion, see WM, 2:79.)

Anchor (6:19)

We get our English word from the Greek noun *angkyran*. This is found three times in Acts (27:29, 30, 40) for the anchor of a ship. But here—its only other occurrence in the NT—it is used figuratively for the anchor of the soul, which is hope.

Sure and Stedfast (6:19)

The Greek adjectives are *asphalēs* and *bebaios*. They are practically synonymous. Abbott-Smith defines the former as "certain, secure, safe," and the latter as "firm, secure." *Asphalēs* literally means "not tripped up." The two together suggest "firm and secure" (NIV), which fits well with an anchor.

Veil (6:19)

The Greek word is *katapetasma*. Usually in the Septuagint, and always in the Greek NT, it is used for the inner veil or curtain that separated the holy place from the holy of holies in the Tabernacle and Temple. The NIV spells this out for the reader by saying of hope: "It enters the inner sanctuary behind the curtain," God's dwelling place.

Without Descent (7:3)

This is one word in Greek, *agenealogētos* (only here in NT). It is compounded of *a*-negative and the verb *genealogeō* (found in NT only in v. 6), "to trace ancestry." So it clearly means "without genealogy" (NASB, NIV)—that is, without a recorded pedigree. We should not assume, as some have wrongly done, that Melchizedek was without human ancestry. The same should be said about the added description: "Having neither beginning of days, nor end of life." It means that the dates of his birth and death are unknown.

Made Like (7:3)

The verb *aphōmoioō* (only here in NT) is in the form of a perfect passive participle. The idea seems to be that Melchizedek was like the Son of God in the timelessness of his priesthood: He had no predecessor or successor. J. Schneider says that in the perfect tense, as here, the verb means, "to be like" (TDNT, 5:198).

Carnal (7:16)

The Greek adjective *sarkinos* comes from the noun *sarx,* "flesh." The English word *carnal* (KJV) comes from the Latin word for flesh. But it has taken on a largely pejorative sense, so that it does not fit here, where we are dealing with a matter of "physical requirement" (NASB), or "as to his ancestry" (NIV). Jesus came from the tribe of Judah and so did not meet the requirement of being a physical descendant of Levi (v. 14). Rather, He was a priest in the order of Melchizedek.

Endless (7:16)

The Greek adjective *akatalytos* (only here in NT) is compounded of *a*-negative and the verb *katalyo,* "destroy." So it means "indestructible" (NASB, NIV).

Repent (7:21)

Today we normally use the word *repent* for feeling remorse for sin or some misdeed. The Greek verb here is *meta-melomai*, which usually has that sense. But George Wesley Buchanan points out that this "is formed from the preposition 'after' and the verb 'to care,' 'be anxious about,' 'take thought.' This word, then, means to have an 'after thought' or an 'after care,' to give the matter a second thought." Buchanan concludes, "The claim of both Ps. 110 and the author is that God made a firm decision about this and he would never give it a second thought. It could not come up for reconsideration" (*To the Hebrews,* Anchor Bible, 127). Probably the best translation here is "will not change his mind" (NIV; cf. NASB).

Testament (7:22)

This is the first of 17 times that the word *diathēkē* occurs in Hebrews. In the KJV it is translated "covenant" 11 times and "testament" 6 times.

But this is unfortunate. In his monumental commentary on the Greek text of Hebrews, B. F. Westcott writes, "There is not the least trace of the meaning 'testament' in the Greek Old Scriptures [the Septuagint], and the idea of a 'testament' was indeed foreign to the Jews till the time of the Herods" (p. 299).

The ordinary Greek word for "covenant" was *synthēkē,* which does not occur in the NT. This term indicates an agreement made between two or more parties. The reason the sacred writers chose *diathēkē* is clear: *synthēkē* was used for a covenant made between equals, but God's covenant with mankind is a unilateral agreement: God dictates the terms.

For a further treatment of *diathēkē,* see the discussion at Heb. 9:16-17 and Gal. 3:15.

Surety (7:22)

The word is *engyos* (only here in NT). Jesus is the divine "Guarantee." Preisker suggests that He is the "Guarantor" of the promises of God. He writes, "With his life, death and ascension Jesus has given us the assurance ... that the beginning of the saving work of God will necessarily be followed by its completion" (TDNT, 2:239).

To the Uttermost (7:25)

The Greek phrase *eis to panteles* occurs (in the NT) only here and in Luke 13:11 ("at all"). Westcott says that it means "completely, wholly, to the uttermost" (p. 191). The NIV has "completely," whereas the NASB has "forever." Delling notes that outside the Bible the word *panteles* means "complete," and the phrase signifies "completely" (TDNT, 8:66-67). But he combines the two ideas of the NIV and NASB in this interesting observation: "The One who saves 'for ever' ... is also, however, the One who saves 'altogether,' so that the saying about the 'totality' of the saving work can hardly be expounded in only a single direction" (p. 67).

Consecrated (7:28)

The Greek has *teteleiōmenon,* the perfect passive participle of the verb *teleioō,* "complete" or "perfect." So the correct translation is "made perfect" (NASB, NIV). Jesus is "perfect" in contrast to the Levitical priests who were "weak" (NASB, NIV).

Sum (8:1)

The word *kephalaion* comes from *kephalē,* "head." In the only other place in the NT where it occurs (Acts 22:28) it means "sum" (of money)—see discussion there (WM,

2:145). But here it has its primary meaning, "main point" (NASB).

Is Set (8:1)

In the KJV the verb *kathizō* is correctly translated "sat down" twice in Hebrews (1:3; 10:12). But here and in 12:2 it is given the awkward, incorrect rendering "is set."

Of the Sanctuary (8:2)

The Greek literally says "of the holy things" *(tōn hagiōn)*. But here and in 9:1 the adjective is used as a substantive (neuter sing. in 9:1) for the "sanctuary" of the Tabernacle.

Example (8:5)

The term *hypodeigma* was used in secular Greek for an "example." But it also meant "copy." That meaning fits better here and in 9:23 (NASB, NIV). In the latter passage the KJV has "pattern(s)."

Mediator (8:6)

See the discussion at 1 Tim. 2:5 (WM, 5:179-81).

Made ... Old ... Decayeth (8:13)

Both of these translate the same verb, *palaioō,* which comes from the adjective *palaios.* Arndt and Gingrich say that the adjective means "*old* = in existence for a long time, often with the connotation of being antiquated or outworn" (*Lexicon,* 605). Seesemann writes, "The word has theological significance only in Hb. 8:13, where it occurs twice. . . . the author argues . . . that by setting up the new covenant

God has declared the old to be outdated. God himself cancels its validity" (TDNT, 5:720).

Since it is the same verb in 13*a* and 13*b*, it is best to translate: "made obsolete" and "is becoming obsolete" (NASB; cf. NIV). The first form is the perfect active indicative, and the second is the present passive participle. With the coming of the new covenant in Christ, the old covenant made at Sinai is now obsolete. We are not under law but under grace.

Waxeth Old (8:13)

This is the present active participle of the verb *gēraskō* (in NT only here and John 21:18), which comes from the noun *gēras*, "old age" (only in Luke 1:36). It means "growing old" (NASB) or "aging" (NIV).

Candlestick (9:2)

The Greek word is *lychnia*, which means "lampstand" (NASB, NIV). They did not use candles in the Tabernacle. See discussion at Matt. 5:15 (WM, 1:19).

Sanctuary (9:2)

It is true that we have here the neuter plural *(Hagia)* of the adjective *hagios*, "holy." But the translation "sanctuary" does not fit here, because verses 2 and 3 describe two sanctuaries. The first (v. 2) was called "the Holy Place" (NIV; cf. NASB). The second (v. 3), behind the inner curtain, was called "the Most Holy Place" (NIV). The Greek is *Hagia Hagiōn*—literally, "the Holy of Holies" (NASB). These two rooms together comprised one building, which could be referred to as "The Sanctuary." The rest of the Mosaic Tabernacle consisted of open courts or courtyards.

The Shewbread (9:2)

In the NT this same term occurs (in KJV) in each of the Synoptic Gospels (Matt. 12:4; Mark 2:26; Luke 6:4). There it is a translation of *tous artous tēs prothēseos* —literally, "the loaves of the presentation" (or, "placing before"). Here the order of the words is reversed: *hē prothesis tōn artōn.* This poses a bit of a problem. Maurer suggests, "When Hb. 9:2 lists not only the table but more specifically *hē prothesis ton arton* as an object in the temple sanctuary, the reference is not so much to the act of placing as to something concrete, perhaps the bread laid on the table . . ." (TDNT, 8:165).

Cherubims (9:5)

This is the only place in the NT where this term occurs, though it is found scores of times in the OT. It comes directly from the Hebrew *kerubim. Im* is the masculine plural ending of Hebrew nouns. So to say "cherubims" (KJV) is simply not correct; it is like saying "I have three childrens." All good modern versions, of course, have correctly "cherubim" or "cherubs."

Figure (9:9)

It comes as a bit of a surprise to discover that the Greek word here is *parabolē,* which is translated "parable" (KJV) 46 out of the 50 times it occurs in the NT. It is used for the parables of Jesus 17 times in Matthew, 13 times in Mark (though translated "comparison" in 4:30), and 17 times in Luke. Once in the Synoptic Gospels it is rendered as "proverb" (Luke 4:23). Aside from these Gospels it is found only in Hebrews (9:9; 11:19)—where the KJV has "figure."

The noun *parabolē* comes from the verb *paraballō,* which means "place beside," "compare." Here it may well be translated "illustration" (NIV), which is what the parables were.

Reformation (9:10)

Diorthōsis (only here in NT) comes from the verb *diorthoō*, "set on the right path." Here it is used for the "new order" (NIV), which replaced the old order found in the Mosaic law—as the first part of this verse indicates.

To Come (9:11)

This translation (KJV) is also found in the NASB. But the NIV has: "that are already here." Why the difference?

The simple answer is that the manuscript evidence, including the very earliest Greek manuscripts, goes both ways. Vaticanus (supported by third-cent. Papyrus 46) has *genomenōn*, "have come." But the other fourth-century manuscript, Sinaiticus, has *mellontōn*, "about to be." The fifth-century manuscripts are similarly divided. So we cannot be sure which was the original reading. Actually, both make good sense. We already enjoy the "good things" in Christ, our High Priest. But we shall also enjoy them even more in the time "to come," in heaven. In this case, we can "have our cake and eat it too"!

Building (9:11)

The Greek has *ktiseōs*, which means "creation" (NASB, NIV). The ancient Tabernacle was the place where God manifested His presence among His people. Now the "greater and more perfect tabernacle," not a part of this earthly creation, is where He manifests His presence. This spiritual tabernacle is where Christ ministers as our High Priest.

Testament (9:16-17)

For a full discussion of whether *diathēkē* should be translated as "covenant" or "testament," see our treatment at Gal. 3:15 (WM, 4:197-99). We would agree with most commentators that the only place where this word means "testament" is Heb. 9:16-17.

The reason for this decision is that here we have an emphasis on the death of the one who made the *diathēkē* (v. 16), with an added statement that it is not in force until then (v. 17). This would not be true of a "covenant," but it is true of a "will" (NIV). The latter term is our usual word for what is legally known as "last will and testament."

Shedding of Blood (9:22)

This is one word in Greek, *haimatekchysia* (only here in NT). Apart from this passage, the term is found only in the Early Church fathers. Behm says that it refers here to "the shedding of blood in slaying" (TDNT, 1:176). He goes on to say:

> The main point is that the giving of life is the necessary presupposition of the remission of sins. This was prefigured in the animal sacrifices of the OT, but what could not be actualized in the OT (Heb. 10:4) has now been established as an eternal truth by the death of Christ *(p. 177)*.

Remission (9:22)

The noun *aphesis* comes from the verb *aphiēmi,* which meant "let go, send away," and then "cancel, remit, or pardon" a debt or sin. The noun was used in secular Greek and in the Septuagint for "release" from captivity. Then it came to be used for *"pardon,* cancellation of an obligation, a punishment, or guilt" (AG, 125). Occurring 17 times in the NT, it is translated (KJV) 9 times as "remission" and 6 times as "forgiveness." The latter is more contemporary (NASB, NIV).

Figures (9:24)

The word *antitypos* occurs (in NT) only here and in 1 Pet. 3:21. Interestingly, it is used there in the opposite sense from the way it is employed here.

Strictly speaking, *antitypos* is an adjective meaning "corresponding to." But here it is used as a substantive. Goppelt writes: "In Neo-Platonism, though not in Plato himself, *antitypos* denotes the sensual world of appearance in constrast to the heavenly world of ideas, the *authenticon*" (TDNT, 8:248). He would translate *antitypa* (pl.) here as "counterpart" (p. 258).

Though we get our word *antitype* directly from this Greek term, that English word would not fit here. For us, *antitype* means the original. Here *antitypos* means "copy" (NASB, NIV).

The Holy Place (9:25)

It is true that the Greek simply has *ta hagia* (literally, "the holy things"). But we know from the OT that the high priest once a year, on the Day of Atonement, entered "the Most Holy Place" (NIV).

Appointed (9:27)

Ten different Greek verbs are translated "appoint" in the NT (KJV). Only here is *apokeimai* rendered that way. In Luke 19:20 it is used in its literal sense of "laid up" (KJV) or "laid away" (NIV). In the two other places in the NT where it occurs (Col. 1:5 and 2 Tim. 4:8) it is used for spiritual things "laid up" for the Christian. Here in Hebrews the thought is: "Just as man is destined to die once" (NIV).

Sanctified (10:10)

Is it "sanctified" (KJV, NASB) or "made holy" (NIV)? The answer is that both are correct. The Greek verb is *hagiazō,* which comes from the adjective *hagios,* "holy," and the causative *z.* So the literal meaning of *hagiazō* is "make holy." Our familiar word *sanctify* comes from the Latin *sanctus,* "holy," and *ficare,* "to make." So it means "make holy."

Iniquities (10:17)

The Greek word is *anomia.* It is compounded of *a*-negative and *nomos,* "law." So it means "lawless deeds" (NASB) or "lawless acts" (NIV).

Faith (10:23)

The Greek word is not *pistis,* "faith," but *elpis,* "hope" (RSV, NASB, NIV).

Provoke (10:24)

The first meaning of this word today, as given in the *Am. Heritage Dict.* (p. 1054), is "To incite to anger or resentment." Obviously that doesn't fit here. The correct translation is "to stimulate" (NASB) or "spur one another on" (NIV).

If We Sin Wilfully (10:26)

This might be taken to mean that if a person committed one willful sin after being converted, there would be no more atoning sacrifice for his sins. But the verb "sin" is here in the present participle of continuous action. So the correct translation is "If we go on sinning willfully" (NASB) or "If we deliberately keep on sinning" (NIV).

Done Despite (10:29)

This is one word, *enybrisas,* which means "has insulted" (NASB, NIV). The verb *enybrizō* occurs only here in the NT.

Fight (10:32)

The Greek word is *athlēsis* (only here in NT), from which we get our word *athletics.* It comes from the verb *athleō,* which meant to contend in games or athletic contests. So the noun properly means "contest" (NIV).

Afflictions (10:32)

The Greek word here is not at all the one that is usually (and correctly) translated "affliction" in the KJV. Rather, it is the plural of *pathēma,* which means "suffering" (NIV; cf. NASB). The usual word for "affliction" is *thlipsis,* which occurs in the plural in verse 33.

Whilst Ye Were Made a Gazingstock (10:33)

This is all one word in Greek, the present participle of the verb *theatrizō* (only here in NT), which means "expose publicly" (AG; cf. NIV). We get our word *theater* from it.

Spoiling (10:34)

Today this word suggests the spoiling of food. The Greek noun is *harpagē,* which comes from the verb *harpazō*—"steal, carry off, drag away" (AG). Arndt and Gingrich say that the noun is used here for "forcible confiscation of property in a persecution" (p. 108). So the correct translation is "seizure" (NASB) or "confiscation" (NIV).

Patience (10:36)

As we have noted in other places (see on Luke 8:15; 21:19), *hypomonē* does not mean "patience" but "endurance" (NASB) or "perseverance" (cf. NIV).

Translated (11:5)

The Greek verb is *metatithēmi* (twice here), which literally means "convey to another place" (AG). The Greek noun for "translation" is *metathesis,* which has been taken over into English as a chemical term. In the NT it occurs only here and in Heb. 7:12; 12:27.

Today "translate" is used mainly for changing from one language to another. The *Am. Heritage Dict.* gives as its sixth definition: *"Theology.* To convey to heaven without natural death" (p. 1364). That is the way it is used here in the KJV. Today we would say "was taken up" (RSV, NASB) or "was taken from this life" (NIV).

Moved with Fear (11:7)

This is one word in the Greek, the aorist passive participle of *eulabeomai.* In secular Greek this verb was commonly used in the sense of "fear," but it also often has in the Septuagint the idea of "fear of God" (TDNT, 2:752). Bultmann thinks that here it has the sense of "to fear" or have "reverent awe" (p. 753). So we find "in reverence" (NASB) and "in holy fear" (NIV).

Builder and Maker (11:10)

The first noun is *technitēs,* from which we get *technician.* It means "craftsman, artisan, designer" (AG, 814). Arndt and Gingrich suggest for this passage the translation "architect" (NASB, NIV).

The second noun is *dēmiourgos,* which is compounded of *dēmos,* "people," and *ergon,* "work." So it literally means "one who works for the people." Then it came to be used universally in the sense of "builder." The best translation here for the two is "architect and builder" (NASB, NIV).

Abraham (11:11, NIV)

In most translations "Sarah," not "Abraham," is the subject of the entire sentence of this verse. Why does the NIV have "Abraham"?

The main problem with the traditional rendering is the expression "to conceive seed" (KJV). The Greek says "for the laying down of seed" *(eis katabolēn spermatos).* This is the act of a male, not a female, in the reproductive process (see on v. 18).

For this reason, F. F. Bruce suggests that *autē Sarra* be taken as the dative of accompaniment. (The unpointed text of the Greek manuscripts could be taken as either dative or nominative.) Then the verse would read this way: "By faith he [Abraham] also, together with Sarah, received power to beget a child when he was past age, since he counted him faithful who had promised" (*The Epistle to the Hebrews,* in *New International Commentary on the New Testament,* 302). Leon Morris of Australia, in his commentary on Hebrews in the *Expositor's Bible Commentary* (12:119), agrees with this conclusion. These are two leading evangelical NT scholars today. In his *Textual Commentary on the Greek New Testament,* Bruce Metzger concludes on the same note (p. 672).

Offered Up (11:17)

This expression occurs twice in the KJV of this verse, but the Greek has different tenses. In the first instance it is the perfect active indicative of *prospherō*. The perfect tense indicates completed action. But Abraham did not complete his offering up of Isaac (Gen. 22:1-18). A. T. Robertson gives this helpful explanation: "The act was already consummated so far as Abraham was concerned when it was interrupted" (WP, 5:424).

The second occurrence has the same verb, but this time it is in the imperfect tense of action going on. Robertson suggests that here we have "the imperfect of an interrupted action" (ibid). Abraham was in the process of sacrificing his son, but God intervened in time to save the boy.

The distinction between the two tenses is brought out well by changing the second occurrence to "was ready to offer up" (RSV), "was offering up" (NASB), or "was about to sacrifice" (NIV). Incidentally, the verb *prospherō* literally means "bring to." But it is used many times in the NT (more than a dozen times in Hebrews) for offering up sacrifices. That is the meaning here (see NIV).

Seed (11:18)

The Greek word *sperma* has a different meaning here from what it has in verse 11. There it apparently means "semen" (a Latin word that we have taken over into English). Here it has the more common use in NT as "offspring" (NIV) or "descendants." (Cf. A-S, 413, for the distinction in the two verses.)

Figure (11:19)

Strangely, the Greek word is *parabolē*. Occurring 50 times in the NT, it is translated (KJV) 46 times as "parable." But in both occurrences in Hebrews (9:9; 11:19) it is rendered "figure." The phrase *en parabolē*, "in a parable," may be translated "figuratively speaking" (NIV, NASB marg.).

Both (11:21)

The Greek has *hekaston,* which means "each" (NASB, NIV).

When He Died (11:22)

In verse 21 "when he was a dying" ("when he was dying," NIV) is the present participle of the common Greek word for dying, *apothnēskō.* But in verse 22 it is the present participle of *teleutaō.* This verb comes from the noun *telos,* "end," and therefore means "coming to an end." It is used in the NT frequently for dying. But "when he died" (KJV) does not correctly translate the present participle. It should be "when he was dying" (NASB).

Departing (11:22)

The Greek word is *exodos,* which we have taken over into English as "exodus." It literally means "a going out." Since we refer to the escape of the Israelites from Egypt as the Exodus (recorded in the Book of Exodus), it is better to use here "the exodus" (RSV, NASB, NIV).

Proper (11:23)

In the NT the adjective *asteios* is used only twice: here and in Acts 7:20 (see comment there, WM, 2:85). Both times it is applied to the Baby Moses, as it also is in the Septuagint on Exod. 2:2. In Liddell-Scott (p. 260) it is stated that in Exod. 2:2 it meant "pretty, graceful." So in the NASB it is translated "beautiful." The NIV says "no ordinary."

Had Respect (11:26)

The verb is *apoblepō* (only here in NT). It is compounded of *blepō,* "see" or "look," and *apo,* "away from."

Abbott-Smith says it means "to look away from all else at one object" (p. 48). It is the imperfect tense of continuous action. So it is rightly translated "was looking" (NASB) or "was looking ahead" (NIV).

Recompence of the Reward (11:26)

This is all one word in Greek, *misthapodosia,* found only in Hebrews (2:2; 10:35; 11:26). In all three places it is translated as above in the KJV. It is compounded of *misthos,* "wages," and the verb *apodidōmi,* "give back." So it was used primarily for the payment of wages, and then for "reward." Here it is used for the "reward" that comes to those who obey God's will. In 2:2 it refers to the "punishment" (NIV) that people receive for disobedience. But here and in 10:35 it is the reward that God's people get for their faithfulness.

Believed Not (11:31)

The Greek verb is *apeitheō,* which definitely means "disobey" or "be disobedient." If the writer had meant "believed not," he would have used *apisteō* (from *pistis,* "faith"). Appropriately, Marvin Vincent says *apeitheō* indicates "disbelief as it manifests itself in disobedience" (WS, 4:531). The correct translation is "disobedient" (RSV, NASB, NIV).

Subdued (11:33)

The verb is *katagōnizomai* (only here in NT), a perfective compound meaning to "struggle against," and then "conquer" (cf. RSV, NASB, NIV).

Were Tempted (11:37)

It is impossible to know today whether this (one word in Greek, *epeirasthēsan*) was, or was not, in the original Greek text. In our oldest manuscript of Hebrews (Papyrus 46, from about A.D. 200) it does not occur. The expression is retained in the NASB, but not in the NIV.

Provided (11:40)

The verb is *problepō* (only here in NT). It literally means "see beforehand" *(pro),* and so here "foreseen" (RSV, NASB marg.). Arndt and Gingrich suggest "provided" for this passage. God not only foresaw but "planned" (NIV).

Weight (12:1)

The noun *ogkos* (only here in NT) literally means a "weight" or "burden," and so metaphorically an "encumbrance" (NASB). The NIV spells it out as "everything that hinders."

Which Doth So Easily Beset (12:1)

This is all one word in Greek, *euperistatos* (only here in NT). Westcott adopts the sense "readily encircling, besetting, entangling" (p. 394). Probably the best rendering is "so easily entangles" (NASB, NIV). Marcus Dods suggests that the reference is to "that which characterises all sin, the tenacity with which it clings to a man" (EGT, 4:365). So we would suggest also the rendering: "the sin which clings so closely to us."

Patience (12:1)

Once more (see comment on 10:36) we note that *hypomonē* does not mean "patience" (KJV). No one ever won a race by patience. It takes "endurance" (NASB) or "perseverance" (NIV). This is a lifelong, long-distance race.

Looking (12:2)

The verb *aphoraō* (only here and Phil. 2:23) means "to look away from all else at, fix one's gaze upon" (A-S, 71-72). So we find "fixing our eyes" (NASB) and "Let us fix our eyes" (NIV). Keeping our eyes fixed on Jesus is the only safe way to live in a sinful world. This involves looking "away from all else" that would turn us aside.

Finisher (12:2)

The noun *teleiōtēn*—found only in later Christian writers, after this occurrence (TDNT, 8:86)—comes from the verb *teleioō,* which literally means "bring to an end" *(telos),* and so "make complete or perfect." Probably the best translation here is "perfecter" (NASB, NIV).

Contradiction (12:3)

The word *antilogia* literally means "a speaking against." But in Jude 11 it clearly indicates a "rebellion" (NASB, NIV). So here it may mean "hostility" (NASB), a meaning found in the secular papyri of the NT period, or simply "opposition" (NIV).

Chastening, Chasteneth, Chastisement (12:5-11)

"Chastening" (vv. 5, 7, 11) and "chastisement" (v. 8) translate the Greek noun *paideia.* "Chasteneth" (vv. 6, 7) and "chastened" represent the verb *paideuō.* All of these are based on the word *pais,* "child." So they all refer to child training. Today we call this "discipline," which conveniently acts as both verb and noun. So the NASB and NIV correctly use "discipline." This includes verse 9, where the KJV has "corrected." The Greek has *paideutas,* "one who disciplines" (here in the pl.).

While we are looking at this section on child discipline, we should like to make one observation: It is difficult to see how any reasonable-minded person could defend the reading aloud of the KJV of verse 8. The fact that the offensive term there was an acceptable word in that period (1611) does not make it so now. Even to give an innocent child or young person a copy of the "The Holy Bible" with that "dirty word" in it can create unnecessary problems. The Greek simply says *nothoi,* "illegitimate children" (RSV, NASB, NIV).

Follow (12:14)

The Greek word that actually means "follow" is *akoloutheō.* But we have here a much stronger term, *diōkō,* which means "pursue." It is used in classical Greek for an animal pursuing its prey, as a hound dog on the trail of a fox—pursuing all day! So we must "pursue" peace with all people, and holiness—literally, "the sanctification" (NASB)—as long as we live.

Morsel of Meat (12:16)

The KJV constantly uses "meat" for all kinds of food, whereas today the term is used only for "edible flesh" (*Am. Heritage Dict.,* 812). In the Greek, "morsel of meat" is just one word, *brōsis,* which literally means "eating." So the correct translation is "a single meal" (NASB, NIV).

Birthright (12:16)

The Greek word is *prōtotokia* (only here in NT), which is compounded of *prōtos,* "first," and *tiktō,* "give birth." So a more adequate translation is "inheritance rights as the oldest [firstborn] son" (NIV). The firstborn son was entitled to a double portion of the family estate.

Repentance (12:17)

The Greek word *metanoia,* as we have noted before, literally means a "change of mind" (NIV). A. T. Robertson says that "it" (which Esau sought with tears) was "the blessing" (see NIV)—not repentance. Robertson adds: "There was no change of mind in Isaac" (WP, 5:438). Esau was not seeking repentance, but to change his father's mind.

An Innumerable Company (12:22)

This is all one word in Greek, the plural of *myrias,* "myriad" (cf. NASB). We get our word *myriad* from the genitive case, *myriados.* It literally means "ten thousand," and so "thousands upon thousands" (NIV). Here it is used hyperbolically for "vast numbers" (A-S, 298; cf. KJV).

To the General Assembly (12:23)

This is one word in Greek, *panēgyrei,* the dative case of *panēgyris* (only here in NT), which meant a "festal assembly" (A-S, 335). In the Greek text this is the final word of verse 22—see NIV, "in joyful assembly"—not the beginning of verse 23.

Written (12:23)

We have here the perfect passive participle of *apographō.* In the only other places in the NT where it occurs (Luke 2:1, 3, 5), this verb means "enroll" for a census. So here it may be translated "enrolled" (NASB) or "names are written" (NIV).

Mediator (12:24)

See comments on 1 Tim. 2:5 (WM, 5:179-81).

Let Us Have Grace (12:28)

The Greek is *echōmen charin*. The noun *charis* does usually mean "grace" in the NT. But in Luke 17:9 the combination, as here, with the verb *echō*, "have," is translated "thank" (KJV, NASB, NIV). "Thanks" and "gratitude" are listed in Greek lexicons as one meaning of *charis*. So here we have "let us show gratitude" (NASB) or "let us be thankful" (NIV).

Brotherly Love (13:1)

The Greek word is *philadelphia* (see comments on 1 Thess. 4:9, WM, 5:133-34).

In Bonds (13:3)

The Greek noun *desmios* comes from the verb *deō*, "bind." So it does mean one who is bound. But it is the regular word for "prisoner" (cf. NASB, NIV). Many Christians were Roman prisoners at this time.

Is (13:4)

This word is in italics (KJV), indicating that there is no verb in the Greek text. The rather obvious meaning of the passage is brought out much better in the NASB—"Let marriage be held in honor among all, and let the marriage bed be undefiled"—or the NIV—"Marriage should be honored by all, and the marriage bed kept pure." In numerous places we have to add a verb to make any sense in English.

Whoremongers (13:4)

This is not acceptable contemporary English. The Greek word *pornos* may be translated "fornicator" (cf.

NASB), a term not commonly used today. Actually it means "the sexually immoral" (NIV).

The second noun, *moichos,* does mean "adulterer." For the sake of English style the NIV has reversed the order of these terms.

Conversation (13:5, 7)

See comments at Gal. 1:13 (WM, 4:179-80).

Without Covetousness (13:5)

The Greek adjective *aphilargyros* (only here and in 1 Tim. 3:3) literally means "without love of money." So it is best translated "free from the love of money" (NASB, NIV).

Which Have the Rule (13:7)

This is the present participle of *hēgeomai,* which primarily means "lead" (cf. NASB), and so "rule" (KJV). Abbott-Smith gives for the present participle: "a ruler, leader." The NIV has adopted the latter as more appropriate for "leaders" in the church (also in vv. 17, 24).

Divers (13:9)

This is Old English for "diverse." The Greek adjective *poikilos* means "variegated," and so "varied" (NASB) or "all kinds of" (NIV).

Meats (13:9)

The Greek word *brōma* means "food." Here the idea clearly is "ceremonial foods" (NIV) in the Mosaic ritual.

Communicate (13:16)

We use "communicate" now mostly for speaking or

writing some message. The Greek word here is *koinōnia*, which means "fellowship" or "sharing." The latter fits the context here.

Make You Perfect (13:21)

The verb *katartizō* means "furnish completely" or "equip." Probably the latter (NASB, NIV) fits best in this sentence.

Set at Liberty (13:23)

As this was from prison, we would say "released" (NASB, NIV).

JAMES

James (1:1)

The Greek form is *Iakōbos*, "Jacob." This James, the brother of Jesus (as most scholars hold), was named after Jacob (Israel), the father of the 12 tribes of Israel.

Scattered Abroad (1:1)

The Greek has *en tē diaspora*, "in the Diaspora"—technical name for the Dispersion of Jews in the Assyrian and Babylonian captivities and from then till the time of Christ. The Jews became "dispersed abroad" (NASB) or "scattered among the nations" (NIV). This Epistle was written primarily to Jews.

Temptations (1:2)

The Greek noun is *peirasmos*. It can be, and is, translated "temptation" in some other places. But the context here suggests "trials" (NASB, NIV).

Patience (1:3-4)

As we have noted before, *hypomenē* means "endurance" (NASB) or "perseverance" (NIV).

Wavereth (1:6)

This is the present passive participle *diakrinomenos,* as also in the previous clause—"nothing" (literally "not at all," *mēden*) "wavering." The verb *diakrinō* literally means "judge between." But in Hellenistic Greek (NT) it came to mean "To be divided in one's mind, to hesitate, doubt" (A-S, 108). So the best translation in this verse is: "without any doubting" and "the one who doubts" (NASB; cf. NIV). Buechsel writes: "Jm. 1:6 gives a vivid description of the man of prayer who is a *diakrinomenos.* He does not stand firm on the promise of God but moves restlessly like a wave of the sea" (TDNT, 3:947).

That Endureth Temptation (1:12)

The Greek is *hypomenei peirasmon.* The verb *hypomenō* is, of course, related to the noun *hypomonē* (v. 3). So the best translation is "who perseveres under trial" (NASB, NIV).

When He Is Tried (1:12)

The Greek *dokimos genomenos* is literally "having become approved"—as a result of having been tested. So it may be translated "once he has been approved" (NASB) or "when he has stood the test" (NIV).

Cannot Be Tempted (1:13)

The Greek says that God is *apeirastos.* This adjective (only here in NT) is compounded of *a*-negative and the verb *peirazō,* "tempt" (which occurs three times in v. 13 and once in v. 14). Literally the statement is that God is "untemptable" by evil.

Enticed (1:14)

This is the present passive participle of *deleazō* (in NT only here and 2 Pet. 2:14, 18). It comes from the noun *delear,* "a bait." So it meant to catch fish by bait. Evil desires act as a bait to "hook" us and get us in trouble.

Superfluity of Naughtiness (1:21)

The first word is *perisseia,* which means "abundance"; the second noun is the very common term *kakia,* "badness." But in the moral sense, as here, it means "wickedness, depravity." Arndt and Gingrich translate the combination here: "excess of wickedness."

Engrafted (1:21)

The word is *emphyton* (only here in NT). It means "rooted, implanted" (A-S, 150), rather than "engrafted." God's Word is to be rooted in our hearts.

Natural (1:23)

The Greek says "the face of his *genesis*"—literally "beginning," and so "birth." That would be his "natural face."

Glass (1:23)

The Greek noun *esoptron* occurs only here and in 1 Cor. 13:12. In those days mirrors were not made of glass but of metal (usually copper or tin). So the correct translation is "mirror."

Religious (1:26)

In the Greek this is a noun, *thrēskos* (only here in NT), used as a predicate adjective. A. T. Robertson notes that "it refers to the external observances of public worship, such as church attending, almsgiving, prayer, fasting" (WP, 6:24). He adds: "It is the Pharisaic element in Christian worship."

Religion (1:26, 27)

The noun is *thrēskeia* in both places. In verse 26 it carries its primary sense of outward observances, but in verse 27 it seems to include more. It consists not only of righteous acts but also of pure character.

Of Our Lord (2:1)

This is clearly not a subjective genitive (Jesus' believing) but objective genitive—people believing in Jesus. So the correct translation is not "of" (KJV) but "in" (NASB, NIV).

Respect of Persons (2:1)

This is one word in Greek, *prosōpolēmpsiais*. See discussion at Rom. 2:11 (WM, 3:55). It means "favoritism" (NIV) or "personal favoritism" (NASB).

Assembly (2:2)

The Greek word is *synagōgē*, which is compounded of *syn*, "together," and *agō*, "gather." So it literally means a "gathering together," and so "assembly" (KJV, NASB) or "meeting" (NIV). James is the only NT writer who uses this for a Christian gathering. That was because he was writing to Jews (see discussion at 1:1). Elsewhere in the NT *ecclēsia*, "church," is used.

Vile (2:2)

The Greek word *hrypara* means "filthy, dirty" (A-S, 399). And in the *Oxford English Dictionary* (12:201) the first definition given is "despicable on moral grounds." But Tyndale, in the first printed English NT, used "vyle" here and so it got into KJV, which retained most of Tyndale. Today we would say "dirty" (NASB) or "shabby" (NIV).

Of (2:4)

"Judges of evil thoughts" (KJV) would suggest judging the evil thoughts of others. But the clear meaning of this passage is "judges with evil thoughts" (NIV). "Thoughts" *(dialogismōn)* is literally "reasonings" (NASB marg.).

Despised (2:6)

The verb *atimazō* is compounded of *a*-negative and the noun *timē,* "honor." So it literally means "dishonor" (cf. NASB). Abbott-Smith also gives "insult" (cf. NIV).

Ye Have Respect to Persons (2:9)

This is one word in Greek, the verb form *prosōpolēmpteite* (cf. noun in v. 1). The NIV helpfully uses "show favoritism" in both places.

Convinced (2:9)

The verb *elengchō* was a technical legal term in the first century, used for being convicted in court. So the proper translation here is "convicted by the law" (NASB, NIV).

Can Faith (2:14)

In the first question of the verse *pistis,* "faith," stands

alone. But in the second question it has the definite article
(hē). This is brought out by "that faith" (NASB) or "such
faith" (NIV). We are saved through faith, but not by a faith
that has no good works or deeds.

Naked (2:15)

The adjective *gymnos* does mean "naked." But in classical Greek it is used frequently in the sense of "scantily or
poorly clad" (A-S, 96). Oepke says that here it means "badly
clothed" (TDNT, 1:773-74).

Devils (2:19)

The Greek word is *daimonia,* from which we get "demons." There is only one "devil" *(diabolos),* but there are
many demons.

Out of the 60 times that *daimonion* (sing.; pl. *daimonia*)
occurs in the NT, it is translated "devil(s)" in the KJV 59
times (once, "god," Acts 17:18). This is unfortunate. The
distinction should always be made.

Masters (3:1)

The Greek has *didaskaloi,* "teachers" (from *didaskō,*
"teach"). Though the KJV always translates the verb as
"teach" (97 times), it renders the noun *didaskalos* (sing.) as
"master" 7 times when it does not refer to Jesus. (The NIV
uses "Master" for Jesus.) But aside from "Master" for Jesus
(40 times), the term "master" in the NT usually refers to a
slave master, which is the usage we are accustomed to today.
So here the better translation is "teachers" (NASB, NIV).

We Offend All (3:2)

This is not a true statement, and the Greek does not
have it. "All" is not in the accusative (objective) case but in

the nominative *(hapantes)*. So it is the subject of the verb, not the object. We do not offend all people, but we do all offend.

The verb "offend" here is *ptaiō* (found also in 2:10). Its regular meaning is "stumble." In this chapter James is speaking particularly about the tongue (vv. 1-12). Honesty compels us to say that in our speech "we all stumble in many ways" (NASB, NIV). Connecting this verse with the admonition of the previous verse, J. H. Ropes makes this interesting observation: "All men stumble, and of all faults those of the tongue are the hardest to avoid. Hence the profession of teacher is the most difficult mode of life conceivable" (ICC, James, 228).

Bridle (3:2)

The verb is *chalinagōgeō* (only here and 1:26 in NT). It literally means to "lead with a bridle" (*agō*, "lead," plus *chalinos*, "bridle," as in v. 3). Here it is used metaphorically in the sense of "bridle" or "restrain." It means "keep . . . in check" (NIV).

Governor (3:4)

Today we do not speak of the "governor" of a ship. The Greek has the present participle of the verb *euthynō* (only here and John 1:23). Literally it is "the one directing or steering." This would be "the pilot" (NASB, NIV).

Listeth (3:4)

The Greek is *bouletai,* which means "wishes" or "desires" (NASB).

Matter (3:5)

The Greek word here, *hylē* (only here in NT), literally meant a "forest." It is true that Greek philosophers, such as Aristotle, used it in the sense of "matter," and the KJV translators were influenced by this fact. But "forest" (RSV, NASB, NIV) fits perfectly.

How Great . . . a Little (3:5)

We have here a very interesting phenomenon: Both of these expressions translate the same Greek adjective! *Hēlikos* properly means "how great." But as used here doubly in the interrogative it means "how great . . . how small" (A-S, 199). The NIV expresses it well: "what a great forest is set on fire by a small spark"—such as a smoldering cigarette stub!

Body (3:6)

For this word (NIV, "person") see the discussion at Rom. 12:1 (WM, 3:213).

Course (3:6)

The Greek noun *trochos* (only here in NT) comes from the verb *trechō*, "run." It was the Greek word for "wheel" (KJV marg.). This may suggest the whole "round" of life.

Nature (3:6)

The Greek word is *genesis*, which literally means "beginning." But here it seems to mean "existence" or "life" (NASB, NIV). That makes the best sense in this passage: "course of life." Incidentally, all commentators recognize this as a difficult verse to interpret.

Unruly (3:8)

The Greek *akatastaton* (only here and 1:8) is compounded of *a*-negative and the verb *kathistēmi*, "set down" or "set in order." In 1:8 it is translated "unstable" (KJV, NASB, NIV). But here it is perhaps best rendered as "restless" (NASB, NIV). That's what our tongues are!

Deadly (3:8)

The adjective *thanatēphoros* (only here in NT) is compounded of *thanatos*, "death," and the verb *pherō*, "bear." So it means "death-bearing."

Place (3:11)

The Greek word is more definite than this. *Opē* (only here and Heb. 11:38) literally means "hole" and is so translated (pl.) in the Hebrews passage (NASB, NIV). Here it means "opening" (NASB).

Endued with Knowledge (3:13)

This is one word in Greek, *epistēmōn* (only here in NT). It comes from the verb *epistamai*, "know, understand." So the simplest meaning is "understanding" (NASB, NIV).

Conversation (3:13)

This translation (KJV) is entirely incorrect today. The Greek word is *anastrophē*. See discussion at Gal. 1:13 (WM, 4:179-80). Here it means "behavior" (NASB) or "life" (NIV).

Strife (3:14, 16)

Eritheia is found before NT times only in Aristotle, the famous Greek philosopher. He uses it for those who were selfishly seeking political office. Buechsel thinks it is best to understand the word as meaning "base self-seeking" (TDNT, 2:661). This is well indicated by "selfish ambition" (NASB, NIV).

Sensual (3:15)

The Greek adjective is *psychikos*. It can be translated "natural" (NASB), as opposed to the spiritual (A-S, 489). Probably this is best expressed by "unspiritual" (NIV, NASB marg.).

Devilish (3:15)

The Greek adjective is *daimoniōdēs* (only here in NT). The best translation is "demonic" (NASB).

Gentle (3:17)

This is not the usual word for "gentle." It is *epieikēs*. J. B. Mayor says that Thucydides used it of men "who would listen to reason" (p. 131). So it may be translated "reasonable," or "considerate" (NIV).

Easy to Be Entreated (3:17)

Eupeithēs (only here in NT) is compounded of *eu,* "well," and the verb *peithomai,* "be persuaded." So the KJV is a literal translation. It may be rendered "reasonable" (NASB) or "submissive" (NIV).

Wars and Fightings (4:1)

The Greek has *polemoi kai ... machai.* The primary meaning of the first term is "wars," and it is so rendered by NASB and NIV in "wars and rumors of wars" (Matt. 24:6; Mark 13:7). In the singular it is used sometimes for a "battle." A second meaning is figurative, as here, a "conflict" or "quarrel."

The primary meaning of the second noun, *machai,* is "contentions" or "quarrels." Abbott-Smith suggests that here the two terms are equivalent, both indicating "private quarrels" (p. 370). The whole expression may be rendered "quarrels and conflicts" (NASB) or "fights and quarrels" (NIV). The verb forms of these, in reverse order, occur in the middle of verse 2—"quarrel and fight" (NIV).

Lusts (4:1, 3)

The Greek word is *hēdonē,* from which we get *hedonism.* It means, in the plural, "pleasures" (NASB). The verb "lust" (v. 2) is an entirely different term, *epithymeō,* which basically means "desire" or "want" (NIV) but sometimes has the bad connotation "lust" (NASB).

Amiss (4:3)

The Greek adverb is *kakōs,* which literally means "badly." In a moral sense, as here, it means "wickedly" or "with wrong motives" (NASB, NIV).

Adulterers and Adulteresses (4:4)

The oldest Greek manuscripts have only *moichalides,* "adulteresses." The additional masculine form does not appear until the ninth century. The term "adulteress" is here used in the spiritual sense, "friendship with the world" (NASB, NIV), just as Israel in the OT is described as the adulterous wife of the Lord (Jer. 3:20; Hos. 9:1). A later scribe took it in the physical sense and added *moichoi,* "adulterers."

Friendship (4:4)

The Greek word is *philia* (only here in NT). It is related to *philos*, "friend" (also in v. 4), and the verb *phileō*, "love" (with emotion and affection). The Christian must love God with all the heart, and not love the world system with its godlessness.

Be Afflicted (4:9)

The verb is *talaipōreō* (only here in NT). It means "be miserable" (NASB). The cognate noun *talaipōria*, in the plural, is translated "miseries" in 5:1. Elsewhere in the NT the noun occurs only in Rom. 3:16 (sing.), where it is rendered "misery" (KJV, NASB, NIV). The "sinners" and "double minded" (v. 8) should be miserable in their condition and humble themselves before the Lord (v. 10).

Speak Evil Of (4:11)

This expression occurs three times in this verse. The Greek verb is *katalaleō*. It is compounded of *laleō*, "speak," and *kata*, "against." So the meaning is "speak against" (NASB; cf. NIV).

Lawgiver (4:12)

Instead of the usual case of a word being added in the late manuscripts, we have here just the opposite. The early manuscripts (before the ninth cent.) have "Lawgiver and Judge" (NASB, NIV).

The Greek word for "Lawgiver," *nomothetēs*, is found only here in the NT. It is compounded of *nomos*, "law," and the verb *tithēmi*, "place" or "set"; it means one who gives or sets the law. God is the supreme Lawgiver. So we should not speak against the law (v. 11).

It Is (4:14)

The NASB and NIV both have "You are." Why the difference? This is a textual problem. Our oldest and best manuscript of the Epistle of James, Vaticanus (fourth cent.), has *este,* "you are," and so do a number of later manuscripts. The evidence for *estin,* "it is," is much weaker. Since the latter seems more natural as an answer to the question, "What is your life?" it is easier to see how a later scribe would change "You are" to "It is" than follow the reverse procedure. In any case, the meaning is essentially the same.

Howl (5:1)

The Greek has the present participle of the verb *ololyzō* (only here in NT). This is what is called an onomatopoetic word—the sound suggests the sense (like "buzz")—and is claimed by one Greek writer (Theander) to be synonymous with *alalazō.* Heidland says that the verb means "'to make a loud and inarticulate cry' in expression of very great stress of soul." He also notes that it "is found in the LXX in prophecies of judgment" (TDNT, 5:173). The rich will weep and howl at the return of Christ (p. 174) because they have lived for self rather than for Him.

Corrupted (5:2)

The verb is *sepō* (only here in NT). Today we would say "rotted" (NASB, NIV). It is in the perfect tense of completed action. There is nothing permanent or eternal about material "wealth" (NIV).

Cankered (5:3)

The verb is *katioō* (only here in NT). It means "have rusted" (NASB) or "are corroded" (NIV). Gold and silver are worth fabulous sums now, but they will be worth nothing then.

Reaped Down (5:4)

The verb is *amaō* (only here in NT). It means to "mow" fields (cf. NASB, NIV).

Kept Back by Fraud (5:4)

The verb *aphystereō* (only here in NT) simple means "keep back" or "withhold." Withholding wages that were due was labeled a serious sin in the OT. "By fraud" is not in the Greek.

Sabaoth (5:4)

This word occurs in the NT only here and in Rom. 9:29 (in a quotation from the Septuagint). It is generally taken as meaning "hosts" or "armies." J. B. Mayor writes, "Its immediate reference is to the hosts of heaven, whether angels or the stars over which they preside: then it is used more generally to express the Divine Omnipotence" (cf. NIV, "Lord Almighty"). He goes on to say, "The use of this name is one among many indications serving to show that the Epistle is addressed to Jews" (p. 158).

Lived in Pleasure (5:5)

The verb *tryphaō* (only here in NT) comes from the noun *tryphē,* which means "softness, daintiness, luxuriousness." So it may be translated "lived luxuriously" (NASB) or "lived . . . in luxury" (NIV).

Been Wanton (5:5)

Spatalaō (only here and 1 Tim. 5:6) has much the same

meaning. It is best translated "led a life of wanton pleasure" (NASB) or simply "lived . . . in . . . self-indulgence" (NIV).

Husbandman (5:7)

See discussion at Luke 20:9, 10, 14, 16 (WM, 1:260). The word *geōrgos* occurs 19 times in the NT and is always translated "husbandman" in KJV. The correct contemporary translation is "farmer" (NASB, NIV).

Grudge (5:9)

The verb *stenazō* literally means to "sigh" or "groan." Mayor writes, "The word denotes feeling which is internal and unexpressed" (p. 162). J. Schneider agrees with this when he says, "The reference is to inner sighing, not to open complaints" (TDNT, 7:603). This seems evident in Mark 7:34—Jesus "sighed."

Suffering Affliction (5:10)

This is one word in Greek, the noun *kakopatheia* (only here in NT). It is related to the compound verb *kakopatheō*, "suffer misfortune," which is found in verse 13. Michaelis says that the sense of the noun (v. 10) is "enduring affliction." The verb (v. 13) "suggests, not so much the distressing situation as such, but the spiritual burden which it brings with it, and which drives us to prayer" (TDNT, 5:937). The OT prophets were examples of the patient suffering of affliction. And we should follow their example.

Count . . . Happy (5:11)

The verb is *makarizō* (only here and Luke 1:48). It means "consider blessed" (NIV; cf. NASB). It comes from the adjective *makarios*, which occurs (in the pl.) as the first word of each of the beatitudes (Matt. 5:3-10). This adjective was used by classical Greek authors for divinely bestowed blessedness, not human happiness. We can be "blessed" when we don't feel "happy."

Patience (5:11)

We have noted several times that *hypomonē* does not mean "patience" (KJV) but "perseverance" (NIV). Job often showed some lack of patience with his "comforters," but he did display a wonderful perseverance in his faith in God.

Very Pitiful (5:11)

This is a "pitiful" translation, considering the contemporary meaning of that term. It now means "pathetic."

The Greek has the compound word *polysplangchnos* (only here in NT). It is composed of *poly,* "much," and *splangchnon*—literally, "inward parts," but figuratively, "compassion." So the correct translation here is "full of compassion" (NASB, NIV).

Let Him Sing Psalms (5:13)

This is all one word in Greek, *psalletō.* The verb *psallō* originally meant to "pull or twitch" (as a bowstring), then "to play" a stringed instrument with the fingers, and finally "to sing to a harp, sing psalms." In the NT it means "to sing a hymn, sing praise" (A-S, 487).

Faults (5:16)

The late Greek manuscripts have *paraptōmata.* This literally means (in the sing.) "a falling beside" and could be translated as "faults." But all the early manuscripts have *hamartias,* "sins" (NASB, NIV).

Subject to Like Passions as We Are (5:17)

This is two words in the Greek, *homoiopathēs hēmin.* The second word simply means "with us." The first word (only here and Acts 14:15) means "of like feelings or affections" (A-S, 317), or "with the same nature." Michaelis says it denotes "one who finds himself in the same or similar relations, whose attitude or feeling is the same or similar" (TDNT, 5:938). The simplest translations are "with a nature like ours" (NASB) or "just like us" (NIV). The point, of course, is that Elijah was not a super-human being when he prayed so effectively, but was just like us, a human being.

1 PETER

_{◈◈}

Strangers (1:1)

The adjective *parepidēmos* (only here; 2:11; and Heb. 11:13) is composed of *para*, "beside," *epi*, "upon," and *dēmos*, "people." It is consistently translated "strangers" in the NIV in the three places where it occurs.

Scattered (1:1)

This is the noun *diaspora*, "dispersion," which we have already seen in James 1:1. It occurs one other place in the NT (John 7:35). While used of Jews in James 1:1, it refers also to Gentiles here and in John.

Foreknowledge (1:2)

The Greek word (only here and Acts 2:23) is *prognōsis*, which we have taken over into English. *Pro* means "before," and *gnōsis* "knowledge."

Hath Begotten . . . Again (1:3)

The verb *anagennaō* (only here and v. 23) is compounded of *gennaō*, "beget," and *ana*, "again." It stresses the "new birth" (NIV)—"has caused us to be born again" (NASB).

Lively (1:3)

The correct translation of *zōsan* is "living." A. T. Robertson notes, "Peter is fond of the word 'living' (present active participle of *zaō*) as in 1:23; 2:4, 5, 24; 4:5, 6" (WP, 6:81).

Incorruptible (1:4, 23)

The adjective *aphthartos* is compounded of *a*-negative and the verb *phtheirō,* "destroy." So it means "imperishable" (NASB, NIV).

Kept (1:5)

The verb *phroureō* comes from the noun *phrouros,* "guard." So it may be translated as "protected" (NASB) or "shielded" (NIV).

Temptations (1:6)

See discussion at James 1:2.

Trial (1:7)

This is *dokimion,* the neuter singular of the adjective *dokimios* (only here and James 1:3). For a long time this word was not given in any Greek lexicon. One scholar (Winer) declared, "There is no adjective *dokimios.*" But Adolf Deissmann found it in the papyri of that period. He writes, "Hence, then, the adjective *dokimios, proved, genuine,* must be recognized, and may be adopted without misgiving in both New Testament passages" (BS, 260). He suggests here in Peter: "what is genuine in your faith."

Appearing (1:7)

The Greek word is *apocalypsis,* which Peter uses three times in this Epistle (1:7, 13, 4:13). It means "revelation." The reference here is to the Second Coming. At the end of verse 13 exactly the same Greek phrase as here is translated in KJV: "at the revelation of Jesus Christ." The NASB and NIV wisely have it the same in both places.

Gird Up the Loins of Your Mind (1:13)

This is a literal translation of the Greek and represents the way they talked back there. It is almost equivalent to the present expression "tighten your belt."

"Gird up" (literally, "girding up") is the aorist middle participle of the rare verb *anazōnnymi* (only here in NT). A. T. Robertson says that this is a "vivid metaphor for habit of the Orientals, who quickly gathered up their loose robes with a girdle when in a hurry or starting on a journey" (WP, 6:87). What the whole expression means is "Prepare your minds for action" (NIV).

Conversation (1:15)

As we have noted before—see discussion at Gal. 1:13 (WM, 4:179-80)—there are three Greek nouns that are translated "conversation" in the KJV, and not one of them means that, as we use the term today. Peter is especially fond of the noun used here, *anastrophē*. He uses it 8 times (1 Pet. 1:15, 18; 2:12; 3:1, 2, 16; 2 Pet. 2:7; 3:11) out of the 13 times it occurs in the NT (see Gal. 1:13; Eph. 4:22; 1 Tim. 4:12; Heb. 13:7; James 3:13). The Greek word literally means the "turnings about" of life. The correct translation is "conduct" (RSV), "behavior" (NASB), or "all you do" (NIV).

Without Respect of Persons (1:17)

This is all one word in the Greek, the adverb *aprosōpo-lēmptōs*—found nowhere else except in the Epistle of Clement of Rome and the so-called Epistle of Barnabas. It is composed of *a*-negative, *prosōpon*, "face," and the verb *lambanō*, "receive." It means that God judges "impartially" (NASB, NIV).

Foreordained (1:20)

The Greek has the perfect passive participle of *proginōskō*, "know before." It is correctly translated this way (KJV) in 2 Pet. 3:17. Also in Rom. 8:29 the KJV has "did foreknow" and in 11:2 "foreknew." The only other place in the NT where the verb occurs (Acts 26:5) it is used of human beings knowing beforehand.

Bultmann writes, "In the NT *proginōskein* is referred to God. His foreknowledge, however, is an election or foreordination of His people (R. 8:29; 11:2) or Christ (1 Pt. 1:20)" (TDNT, 1:715). We feel, however, that God's foreordination is based on His foreknowledge, and the two should not be confused. The NASB correctly has "foreknown" here.

Unfeigned (1:22)

The Greek adjective is *anypocritos*. It comes from *a*-negative and the verb *hypokrinomai*, "play a part" or "pretend." So the adjective means "sincere" (NASB, NIV)—literally, "unhypocritical."

Evil Speakings (2:1)

The noun is *katalalia* (only here and 2 Cor. 12:20). It is compounded of the verb *laleō*, "talk," and *kata*, "against." It may well be translated "slander" (NASB, NIV).

Newborn (2:2)

The adjective *artigennētos* (only here in NT) is composed of *arti*, "just now," and the verb *gennaō* (pass., "born").

Desire (2:2)

Epipotheō is a strong verb, meaning "long for" (NASB) or "crave" (NIV).

Sincere (2:2)

The adjective *adolos* (only here in NT) is compounded of *a*-negative and *dolos*, "deceit." So it means "sincere." As applied to liquids it meant "genuine" or "pure" (NASB, NIV). It can also be translated "unadulterated" milk.

Of the Word (2:2)

This is one word in the Greek, the adjective *logikos* (only here and Rom. 12:1). In both places it probably means "spiritual" (NASB marg., NIV).

Disallowed (2:4, 7)

Apodedokimasmenon is the perfect passive participle of *apodokimazō*, which means "reject after testing." Christ's contemporaries tested Him, the "living Stone," and then most deliberately rejected Him. So the proper translation here is "rejected" (NASB, NIV).

Lively (2:5)

It is the same adjective as "living" in verse 4 and should, of course, be translated that way.

Chief Corner Stone (2:6)

This is one word in Greek, the adjective *akrogōniaios* (only here and Eph. 2:20), used as a substantive. See discussion there (WM, 4:279).

Be Confounded (2:6)

This is the passive of *kataischynō* and means "be ashamed," or "be put to shame" (NIV).

Stumbling . . . Offense (2:8)

The first word is *proskomma*, the second *skandalon*, from which we get "scandal." A. T. Robertson says of these: "*Proskomma* (from *proskoptō*, to cut against) is an obstacle against which one strikes by accident, while *skandalon* is a trap set to trip one, but both make one fall" (WP, 6:98). (See NIV.)

Peculiar (2:9)

Today "peculiar" is a pejorative term, meaning "odd" or "queer." Unfortunately, this translation has been misused by Christians who gloried in being "peculiar."

The Greek has *laos*, "a people," followed by *eis peripoiē-sin*—literally "a people for possession," that is, "God's own possession" (NASB). The meaning is "precious," rather than "peculiar"!

Conversation (2:12)

See discussion at 1:15.

Ordinance of Man (2:13)

"Of man" is the adjective *anthrōpinos*, which means "human." For us "ordinance" means a law or regulation. But the Greek word here is *ktisis*. In the Septuagint and the NT it means "creation"; that is, "that which has been created."

The NASB translates the expression as "human institution," the NIV as "authority instituted among men." Foerster notes that this verse has "special difficulties"; the exact meaning is not perfectly clear. He suggests that this verse might well be "the title of the whole section 2:13-3:9" (TDNT, 3:1035). In that light, the reference may be to our fellowmen, as God's creation. The main emphasis seems to be on maintaining the proper relationship with all human beings.

Cloke (2:16)

The Greek word *epikalymma* (only here in NT) means "a cover." The idea is that of a "covering" (NASB) or "cover-up" (NIV) "for evil." We are not to misuse our Christian freedom.

Servants (2:18)

The Greek has *oiketai*, from *oikos*, "house." So it means household servants. The reference to "masters" shows that they were "slaves" (NIV).

For Conscience Toward God (2:19)

The Greek word for "conscience" is *syneidēsis*. This comes from the verb *syneidon*, "see together." So the first meaning of *syneidēsis* was "consciousness." Finally, with the Stoics, it developed into the idea of self-judging consciousness, and so "conscience" (A-S, 427).

One problem we have here is that in our text *syneidēsis* is followed immediately by *theou*, "of God." (It is also preceded by *dia*, "on account of" or "because of.") So the NIV, perhaps wisely, translates the whole expression: "because he is conscious of God." This makes good sense.

Glory (2:20)

The Greek word *kleos* (only here in NT) did mean "fame" or "glory." But perhaps the best translation here is "credit" (NASB, NIV).

Buffeted (2:20)

This is a strong Greek verb, *kolaphizō.* It literally means "strike with the fist." So it may be translated "receive a beating" (NIV).

Stripes (2:24)

The word *mōlōps* (only here in NT) means a "wound" received by being beaten. So a better translation here is "wounds" (NASB, NIV). He was horribly wounded that we might be healed!

Bishop (2:25)

The word is *episcopos,* from which we get *episcopal.* The term comes from *scopos,* "a watcher," and *epi,* "upon" or "over." So it meant a "superintendent" or "guardian" or "overseer." It finally, in the church, took over the technical form, "bishop." As our "Shepherd," Jesus is our "Guardian" (NASB) or "Overseer" (NIV).

Be in Subjection (3:1)

For the verb *hypotassō,* see discussion of Eph. 5:21 (WM, 4:333) and the following item on 5:25 (for both sides of the marriage relationship). A better translation here is "be submissive" (NASB, NIV). See also verse 5.

Conversation (3:1, 2, 16)

See discussion at 1:15.

Adorning (3:3)

The Greek has *cosmos,* which occurs 187 times in the NT. In every other place it is translated "world"! But that usual meaning obviously would not fit here. Both NASB and NIV have "adornment."

The earliest meaning of *cosmos* (in Homer and Plato) was "order." The second usage was "adornment," as here alone in the NT. Then it came to be used universally for the "world," or the orderly "universe."

The noun is related to the verb *cosmeō,* which means to "put in order" or "arrange." That's what the ladies do with the help of *cosmetics.* The verb may also be translated "adorn" (Matt. 12:44; Luke 11:25). That is the way it is used here in verse 5.

Plaiting (3:3)

The Greek word *emplokē* (only here in NT) means "braiding" (NASB; cf. NIV).

Meek (3:4)

Praus (in NT only here and Matt. 5:5; 11:29; 21:5) may also be translated "gentle" (NASB, NIV). In Matt. 5:5 the NIV retains "meek" because of the familiarity of this beatitude (contra NASB).

Quiet (3:4)

The adjective *hesychiōs* occurs in the NT only here and in 1 Tim. 2:2—see discussion there (WM, 5:178).

Lord (3:6)

The Greek word *kyrios* occurs about 750 times in the NT. In the KJV it is translated "Lord" 667 times, "lord" 55 times, "master" ("Master") 13 times, "sir" ("Sir") a dozen times, and once each "owner" (Luke 19:33) and "God" (Acts 19:20). As one can see, *kyrios* is used not only for Christ or God, but also for slave masters, husbands (as here), or fathers (Matt. 21:30), and even as just a polite form of address (John 12:21, etc.). In our passage here the NIV has "master."

Amazement (3:6)

The noun *ptoēsis* (only here in NT) comes from the verb *ptoeō* (Luke 21:9; 24:37), which means (in the pass.) "be terrified." So the noun means "terror" or "fear" (NASB, NIV).

Dwell With (3:7)

The Greek has the present participle (used as imperative) of the verb *synoikeō* (only here in NT). It is composed of *syn*, "together," and *oikeō*, "dwell" (from *oikos*, "house"—so, living together in the same house). Today we would say "live with" (NASB, NIV).

Be Pitiful (3:8)

See discussion at James 5:11, third item.

Eschew (3:11)

The verb *ekklinō* means "turn away" (NASB).

Ensue (3:11)

The verb is *diōkō*, which means "pursue." In Heb. 12:14 we are likewise told to "pursue peace."

Followers (3:13)

The Greek has the plural of the noun *zēlōtes* and so means "zealous ones" ("zealots"). Here it may be translated "zealous" (NASB) or "eager" (NIV).

Happy (3:14)

The Greek adjective is *makarios* (see discussion at James 5:11, first item).

Sanctify (3:15)

The verb is *hagiazō*, most commonly translated "sanctify" (literally, "make holy"). It is also used in the sense of "set apart." Since we cannot make God holy, perhaps the best rendering here is "set apart" (NIV; cf. NASB marg.).

The Lord God (3:15)

Instead of *theon*, "God," all the Greek manuscripts earlier than the eight century have *Christon*, "Christ." So the correct reading here is "Christ as Lord" (NASB, NIV).

Suffered (3:18)

The NASB and NIV both have "died" instead of "suffered." Why?

This is a textual problem. *Apethanen*, "died," is found in Papyrus 72 (third cent.), Aleph (fourth cent.), A and C (fifth cent.), and other manuscripts of the eight and ninth centuries, as well as many later manuscripts. On the other hand, *epathen*, "suffered," is the reading in B (fourth cent.) and two manuscripts of the ninth century, as well as a limited number of later ones. The early versions almost all have "died." Actually, of course, Jesus both "suffered" and "died" on the Cross. So the meaning is much the same.

Quickened (3:18)

The verb is *zōopoieō,* which means "made alive" (NASB, NIV). Incidentally, since the Greek makes no distinction with capital letters, we cannot be certain whether to have in this verse "Spirit" (KJV, NIV) or "spirit" (NASB). The latter choice was evidently based on the comparison with "in the flesh" (though the margin has "Spirit").

By Water (3:20)

The Greek has the preposition *dia* with the genitive, which means "through." Noah and his family were not saved "by water." Rather, they were saved "through water" (NIV; cf. NASB)—that is, saved through the Flood, not destroyed in it.

Figure (3:21)

The Greek noun is *antitypon,* which we have taken over as *antitype.* It is an adjective, literally meaning "striking back," but metaphorically (as here) "corresponding to" (NASB). Noah's being saved through the Flood "symbolizes" (NIV) Christian water baptism.

Answer (3:21)

The Greek noun is *eperōtēma* (only here in NT). It comes from the verb *eperōtaō,* "to question," but which later came to mean "to demand of." So the noun took the meaning "a demand." A. T. Robertson comments, "In ancient Greek it never means answer, but only inquiry. The inscriptions of the age of the Antonines use it of the Senate's approval after inquiry" (WP, 6:120). So it may refer here to the "pledge" made by the candidate at his baptism. Since *eis theon* immediately follows *eperōtēma* in the Greek, the NASB has "an appeal to God for a good conscience." We cannot be dogmatic about the exact meaning of the passage but can get help from different versions and even different interpretations.

Arm (4:1)

The verb *hoplizō* (only here in NT) comes from the noun *hoplon,* which is used several times in the NT in the plural for "arms" (weapons). So it is appropriate to translate the verb as "arm yourselves" (aorist middle imperative— right now!).

Mind (4:1)

The regular Greek word for "mind" is *nous.* But here we have *ennoia.* It occurs elsewhere (in NT) only in Heb. 4:12, where it is translated "intents" (KJV). Abbott-Smith defines it as "thought, purpose, design" (p. 155). It is compounded of *en,* "in," and *nous,* "mind." Behm says that the word means: "What takes place in the *nous,* 'deliberation,' 'consideration'" (TDNT, 4:968). So it may be translated "purpose" (NASB) or "attitude" (NIV).

Lasciviousness (4:3)

Aselgeia occurs 10 times in the NT and is translated "lasciviousness" 6 times (KJV). Today we would probably say, "licentiousness." It is well rendered "sensuality" (NASB) or "debauchery" (NIV).

Excess of Wine (4:3)

This is one word in Greek, *oinophlygia* (only here in NT). It is compounded of *oinos,* "wine," and *phlyō,* "bubble up, overflow." We call this "drunkenness" (NASB, NIV).

Excess (4:4)

Anachysis (only here in NT) comes from the verb *anacheō,* "pour out." So it means "a pouring out, overflowing, excess" (A-S, 35). This may be represented by "flood" (NIV).

Riot (4:4)

Today "riot" means "a wild or turbulent disturbance created by a large number of people" (*Am. Heritage Dict.,* 1120). The Greek word here is *asōtia,* from *a*-negative and the verb *sōzō,* "save." Probably the best translation is "dissipation" (NASB, NIV).

Quick (4:5)

See discussion at 2 Tim. 4:1 (WM, 5:249).

Be Sober (4:7)

The verb is *sōphroneō.* See discussion at Rom. 12:3 (WM, 3:216-17).

Watch (4:7)

The verb is *nēphō.* See discussion at 1 Thess. 5:6, second item (WM, 5:140). Probably the best translation here is "self-controlled" (NIV).

Fervent (4:8)

This English adjective is defined as: "Having or showing great emotion or warmth" (*Am. Heritage Dict.,* 485). But the Greek word here, *ektenēs* (only here in NT) has a somewhat different connotation. It comes from the verb *ekteinō,* "stretch out"; so it literally means "stretched out." C. E. B.

Cranfield says that it "suggests rather the taut muscle of strenuous and sustained effort, as of an athlete" (*First Epistle of Peter*, 95). A good translation is "unfailing" (RSV).

Use Hospitality (4:9)

There is no verb here in the Greek, just the adjective *philoxenoi* (pl.). See discussion at 1 Tim. 3:2, second item on page (WM, 5:192). We obviously have to put a verb here. So we may read: "Be hospitable" (NASB) or "Offer hospitality" (NIV).

Minister (4:10-11)

The verb *diakoneō* was used basically for waiting on tables. So it means "serve." It is probably better to use that translation here (NASB, NIV), since the admonition applies to all Christians, not simply to those who "minister" in the pulpit.

Strange . . . Strange (4:12)

The second "strange" is a correct translation of the adjective *xenos*, "strange, unusual." But "think it . . . strange" is the present passive imperative of *xenizō*, which means "be surprised" (NASB, NIV)—a regular sense found in late Greek writers.

Are Partakers Of (4:13)

The verb here, *koinōneō*, means "share" (NASB).

Reproached (4:14)

It is interesting that Arndt and Gingrich define the verb *oneidizō* as "reproach, revile, heap insults upon" (p. 570) and that these three meanings are represented in chronological sequence by KJV, NASB, and NIV.

Happy (4:14)

See discussion at 3:14.

Resteth upon You (4:14)

The rest of the verse is not found in any Greek manuscript earlier than the ninth century and so is properly omitted from scholarly versions today.

A Busybody in Other Men's Matters (4:15)

This is all one word in the Greek, *allotriepiscopos* (only here in NT). It is compounded of *allotrios,* "belonging to another," and *episcopos,* "overseer." Charles Bigg writes: *"Allotrioepiscopos* [received Text spelling] is a word not found elsewhere, and probably coined by St. Peter" (*Epistles of St. Peter and St. Jude,* ICC, 177). It seems to mean "meddler" (NIV; cf. NASB).

House (4:17)

The Greek word *oikos* properly means a "house." But by metonymy it signifies, as here, a "household" (NASB) or "family" (NIV), as Abbott-Smith notes (p. 313).

Scarcely (4:18)

Molis comes from *molos,* "toil." So it means "with difficulty, hardly, scarcely" (A-S, 296). (See NASB, NIV.)

In Well Doing (4:19)

In the Greek this is *en agathopoiia* (only here in NT) and is found at the very end of the verse (see NASB, NIV).

The noun comes from the verb *agathopoieō—poieō*, "do," and *agathos*, "good."

Feed (5:2)

The Greek does not have the verb *boskō*, "feed," but *poimainō*. This comes from *poimen*, "a shepherd." So the correct translation is "Shepherd the flock" (NASB; cf. NIV). This involves more than feeding; it means taking care of the sheep.

Flock (5:2-3)

It is interesting that the Greek word here, *poimnion*, is used in the NT only in a metaphorical sense, for Christians (also Luke 12:32; Acts 20:28-29).

Taking the Oversight (5:2)

This is all one word in Greek, *episcopountes*, the present active participle of *episcopoeō* (only here and Heb. 12:15). It literally means "look upon," and then "visit, care for." The participle may be translated "serving as overseers" (NIV).

By Constraint (5:2)

This is one word in Greek, the adverb *anagkastōs* (only here in NT). It has the force of "because you must" (NIV).

Willingly (5:2)

This is another adverb, *hekousiōs* (only here and Heb. 10:26 in NT). It means "voluntarily" (NASB).

The alert reader may have already discovered that after this word there is an added item in NASB ("according to the will of God") and NIV ("as God wants you to be"). This is because after *hekousiōs* there is an added phrase, *kata theou* ("according to God") in Papyrus 72 (third cent.), Sinaiticus (fourth cent.), A (fifth cent.), a considerable number of later manuscripts, and some early versions. We cannot, at this stage, be absolutely certain as to whether this addition was a part of the original text.

Of a Ready Mind (5:2)

This translates the adverb *prothymōs* (only here in NT), which means "eagerly."

Being Lords (5:3)

This is the present participle of the verb *katakyrieuō*. See discussion at Matt. 20:25 (WM, 1:70).

Heritage (5:3)

The Greek has the plural of the noun *klēros*, which means "a lot"—as in "casting lots" or "drawing lots." But here we have the second stage of its use: "that which is obtained by casting" (A-S, 249). So the correct translation here is "those allotted to your charge" (NASB) or "those entrusted to you" (NIV). It must be remembered that this is addressed to the "elders" in the church (v. 1).

Incidentally, it should be noted that *"Gods"* (KJV) is in italics, indicating that it is not in the Greek. So we omit it.

Chief Shepherd (5:4)

This is one word, *archipoimēn*—only here in NT, though found by Adolf Deissmann in two places elsewhere (LAE, 99-101). It is compounded of *archi*, a prefix "denoting high office and dignity" (A-S, 62), and *poimēn*, "shepherd."

For pastors we would like to suggest a series of three

sermons. The first would be on Psalm 22, depicting the Good Shepherd (John 10) who gives His life for the sheep. The second would be based on Psalm 23, where we see the Great Shepherd (Heb. 13:20) caring for His sheep. The third would be on Psalm 24, the Chief Shepherd in glory.

Crown (5:4)

The Greek word here is not *diadēma* (diadem), the royal crown, but *stephanos,* the victor's crown. See discussion at 1 Cor. 9:25, second item (WM, 4:61).

Fadeth Not Away (5:4)

This is one word, the adjective *amarantinos* (only here in NT). A. T. Robertson notes that this word gave name to the flower "amaranth"—"so called because it never withers and revives if moistened with water and so used as a symbol of immortality" (WP, 6:132).

Be Clothed (5:5)

Egkomobōsasthe is the aorist middle imperative of *egkomboomai* (only here in NT)—"clothe yourselves" (NASB, NIV). The verb comes from the noun *kombos,* "a knot." So *egkombōma* meant "a garment tied on others, especially a frock or apron worn by slaves" (A-S, 128). Robertson suggests that Peter may be thinking of what Jesus did when He tied a towel around His waist and washed the disciples' feet (John 13).

Care (5:7)

The noun is *merimna,* which means "anxiety" (NASB, NIV). "Careth" is the verb *melō,* a different root.

Devour (5:8)

The Greek has the second aorist active infinitive of *katapinō*, "to drink down." Satan would like to grab us and gulp us down!

Afflictions (5:9)

The Greek has the plural of the noun *pathēma*, which means "suffering" (cf. NASB, NIV).

Make (5:10)

This (KJV) appears to be in the form of a request. But the Greek has four verbs, all in the future tense—"will Himself perfect, confirm, strengthen and establish you" (NASB). It is a promise, not a prayer.

The first verb is *katartizō*, which means "render *artios*" (fit or complete). It sometimes means "repair" or "restore" (NIV). Then it took on the ethical sense, "to complete," or "perfect" (NASB).

The second verb is *stērizō*, which metaphorically (as here) means "to confirm, establish." The third is *sthenoō* (only here in NT), "to strengthen." The fourth is *themelioō*. It comes from *themelios*, "foundation." So it means "establish."

I Suppose (5:12)

The Greek has *logizomai*, which was first used for numerical calculation, in the sense of "reckon." Then it came to mean "consider." The best translation here is "regard" (RSV, NASB, NIV).

The Church That Is at Babylon (5:13)

"Church" is not in the Greek. All it has is: "She who is

in Babylon" (NASB, NIV). Some take this as meaning Peter's wife. But most scholars think the reference is to the local church. (*Ecclēsia*, the regular word in the NT for "church," is feminine.)

The identification of "Babylon" is also a matter of dispute. Most take it—rightly, we think—as referring to Rome, where Peter was at this time. It was probably safer for him not to mention Rome as the place where he was.

2 PETER

Divine (1:3, 4)

This is the adjective *theois* (only here [twice] and in Acts 17:29). It comes from the noun *theos,* "God."

Virtue (1:3, 5)

See discussion of *aretē* at Phil. 4:8, third item on page (WM, 5:64-65).

Diligence (1:5)

See discussion of *spoudē* at Rom. 12:11, first item (WM, 3:222). Here the NIV translates the whole phrase: "make every effort" (see also 3:14).

Temperance (1:6)

Egkrateia (only here; Acts 24:25; and Gal. 5:23) should be translated "self-control" (NASB, NIV).

Barren (1:8)

The adjective *argos* comes from *a*-negative and the

noun *ergon*, "work." So it means "idle." It may be translated "useless" (NASB) or "ineffective" (NIV).

Unfruitful (1:8)

The adjective *akarpos* comes from *a*-negative and *karpos*, "fruit." So it means "unfruitful" (KJV, NASB) or "unproductive" (NIV)—since "fruit" is used in KJV for "crops."

And Cannot See Afar Off (1:9)

This is all one word in Greek, *myōpazōn*, the present participle of *myōpazō* (only here in NT). It comes from *myōps*, "shortsighted" (NASB), and so means "nearsighted" (NIV). We get our word *myopia* from this.

Sure (1:10, 19)

The adjective *bebaios* means "firm, secure." Deissmann says that it is used "in the sense of legally guaranteed security" (BS, 109). Peter admonishes Christians ("my brothers"): "Be all the more eager to make your calling and election sure" (NIV)—by abiding in Christ. If we do this, we will "never fall." This implies that if we don't do this, we may fall.

Put . . . in Remembrance (1:12)

This is one word in Greek, the verb *hypomimnēskō*, the intensive compound of *mimnēskō*, "remind." It is also best translated "remind" (NASB, NIV).

Meet (1:13)

This is the adjective *dikaios*, which means "just" or "right" (NASB, NIV).

Tabernacle (1:13, 14)

Skēnōman is from the verb *skēnoō,* "dwell"—used in the papyri for living in a temporary dwelling (A-S, 409). Both the noun and verb come from *skēnē,* "tent." The reference here is obviously to Peter's body (cf. NIV). In the only other place in the NT where *skēnōma* occurs (Acts 7:46), it refers to the Temple as God's dwelling.

Shewed (1:14)

The verb *dēloō* comes from the adjective *dēlos,* "clear." So it here means "made clear" (NASB, NIV).

Endeavour (1:15)

The verb is *spoudazō,* which literally means "make haste." It is interesting to note that of the 11 times it is used in the NT it occurs 3 times in Paul's last letter (2 Timothy) and 3 times in Peter's last letter (2 Peter). Both these men had eager, earnest personalities, and this is reflected in their writings, especially as they approached the end.

Decease (1:15)

The Greek word is *exodos* ("exodus"), which means "departure" (NASB, NIV).

Cunningly Devised Fables (1:16)

The Greek has *sesophismenois mythois.* The verb *sophizō* (in the perf. pass. part. here) comes from the adjective *sophos,* "clever" or "wise." In the only other place where it occurs in the NT (2 Tim. 3:15) it has the good meaning of "make wise." But here it has the bad sense of being a sophist, cleverly inventing false myths.

For the noun *mythos*, see our long discussion at 1 Tim. 1:4 (WM, 5:165-67).

The whole phrase here is best translated "cleverly devised tales" (NASB) or "cleverly invented stories" (NIV).

Majesty (1:16)

The noun *megaleiotēs* (only here; Luke 9:43; and Acts 19:27) means "splendor" or "magnificence." Here, as applied to Christ, it means "majesty."

Excellent (1:17)

Here we have the adjective *megaloprepēs* (only here in NT). Obviously related to the above word, it means "befitting a great person, magnificent, majestic." The combination with "glory" is best represented here as "the Majestic Glory" (NASB, NIV)—a title for Christ.

Dawn (1:19)

The verb *diaugazō* (only here in NT) literally means "shine through."

Day Star (1:19)

This is one word in Greek, *phōsphoros* (only here in NT). It comes from *phōs*, "light," and the verb *pherō*, "bear," and so literally means "light-bringing." This word was applied to Venus as the "morning star" (NASB, NIV). The reference seems to be to the second coming of Christ as the Morning Star of the eternal day to come.

Is of Any Private Interpretation (1:20)

The verb here is *ginetai*, which means "becomes" or "comes about." The word "private" translates *idias*, literally "one's own." The noun for "interpretation" is *epilysis*, from the verb *epilyō*, "loose, solve, explain," and so means "interpretation." Probably the correct meaning here is that "no prophecy of Scripture came about by the prophet's own interpretation" (NIV). Verse 20 seems clearly to demand this. Holy Scripture is of divine origin.

Came (1:21)

The form here, *ēnechthē*, is the aorist passive participle of *pherō*, "bear" or "carry." Charles Bigg translates this "was borne" and explains: "came from heaven to man" (ICC, *Epistles of St. Peter and Jude*, 270).

The Greek of the last part of verse 21 literally reads: "But being borne along *(pheromenoi)* by the Holy Spirit, men spoke from God" (cf. NASB, NIV). This is perhaps the strongest statement in the New Testament regarding the divine origin and authority of the Old Testament Scripture. It stands right alongside 2 Tim. 3:16 in asserting this great truth.

Privily Shall Bring In (2:1)

This is one word in Greek, the verb *pareisagō* (only here in NT). It is a double compound: *agō*, "lead" or "bring"; *eis*, "into" or "in"; *para*, "beside." So it came to mean "bring in secretly," or "secretly introduce" (NASB, NIV).

Damnable (2:1)

This is the genitive case of *apōleia*, "of destruction." This same noun is correctly translated "destruction" in the KJV at the end of this verse and of 3:16. But in the third verse it is rendered "damnation" and in 3:7 "perdition." It should be "destruction" in all those passages. And here the correct translation is "destructive" (NASB, NIV).

Heresies (2:1)

The Greek noun *hairesis* gives us our word *heresy*. It comes from the verb *haireō,* which meant "choose." So the noun first meant "choice." Then it came to mean "what is chosen," and finally "a peculiar opinion" or "heresy." It is used that way here, in 1 Cor. 11:19, and Gal. 5:20.

Lord (2:1)

Here we do not have the common Greek word for "Lord," *kyrios.* Rather we find *despotēs,* which we have taken over as "despot." This Greek noun is applied to Christ (in NT) only here and in Jude 4. The NIV has "sovereign Lord" here and "Sovereign" in Jude 4 (because it is accompanied there by *kyrios*). *Despotēs* indicates complete sovereignty.

Pernicious Ways (2:2)

The Greek noun *aselgeia* (here in pl.) means "licentiousness." A good translation here is "sensuality" (NASB).

Feigned (2:3)

The Greek adjective *plastos* (only here in NT) first meant "formed, molded" (cf. our "plastic"). Then it came to mean "fabricated, feigned," or "made up" (NIV).

Make Merchandise of (2:3)

The verb *emporeuomai* (only here and James 4:13) first meant to "travel," especially for business, and so "trade." Here it means "make a gain of," or "exploit" (NASB, NIV).

Hell (2:4)

There are three Greek words that are translated "hell" in the NT of KJV. The first is *geenna* (Gehenna), which really means "hell" and is so rendered in almost all versions. It occurs 12 times in the NT (7 times in Matthew, 3 times in Mark, and once each in Luke and James).

The origin of this name for hell is very interesting. Gehenna was the Valley of the Son of Hinnom, south of Jerusalem. Ahaz and Manasseh, two wicked kings of Judah, sacrificed their sons there to the heathen god Molech (2 Chron. 28:3; 33:6; Jer. 32:35). Good King Josiah defiled the place (2 Kings 23:10), and it became the city dump, with fires burning on it. Then the Jews made "Gehenna" the name for the final judgment and the place of eternal punishment. Jesus used it that way (11 times).

The second word translated "hell" in the NT (KJV) is *hadēs*. It occurs 11 times in the NT and is translated "hell" 10 of those times (KJV). Once (1 Cor. 15:55) it is "grave." *Hadēs* was the name of the god of the underworld and does not mean the place of everlasting punishment; so it should not be translated "hell." It is used in the NT for the abode of departed spirit. Probably the best procedure is to transliterate the word as "Hades."

Here in 2 Pet. 2:4 we find the third word, *tartarōsas* (only here in NT). It is really the aorist participle of *tartaroō* and so is translated "cast *them* down to hell" (KJV). The verb comes from the noun *tartaros,* used for the dark abode of the wicked dead. In the apocryphal Book of Enoch (20:2) it is used as the place of punishment of the fallen angels (as here in 2 Peter). In English we use the Latin form "Tartarus."

Chains (2:4)

We have another textual problem here. "Chains" (KJV) translates the Greek form *sirais,* found in Papyrus 72 (third cent.) and two ninth-century manuscripts (K, P), as well as the majority of later manuscripts. "Pits" (NASB) is the translation of *sirois,* found in our two fourth-century manuscripts (Aleph, B) and two of the fifth century (A, C). We cannot be certain which was the original form, but the meaning is essentially the same.

Flood (2:5)

The Greek word is *cataclysmos,* which has been taken over into English as "cataclysm." This noun comes from the verb *cataclyzō,* "inundate, deluge" (found only in 2 Pet. 3:6). In the NT the noun is used only for Noah's "flood" (here; Matt. 24:38, 39; and Luke 17:27).

Turning . . . into Ashes (2:6)

This is one word in Greek, *tephrōsas,* the aorist participle of *tephroō* (only here in NT). It comes from the noun *tephra* ("ashes"), which one Greek writer used in describing an eruption of Mount Vesuvius.

Vexed (2:7)

Kataponoumenon is the present passive participle of *kataponeō* (only here and Acts 7:24). The verb means to "wear down" *(kata),* and in the passive to be "oppressed" (NASB) or "distressed" (NIV).

Conversation (2:7)

See discussion of *anastrophē* at 1 Pet. 1:15.

The Wicked (2:7; 3:17)

The adjective *athesmos* (only these two places in NT) is compounded of *a*-negative and *thesmos,* "law" or "custom." So it means "lawless men." Abbott-Smith says that it is used "especially of those who violate the law of nature and conscience" (p. 11).

Vexed (2:8)

This is a different verb from the one translated "vex" (KJV) in verse 7. Here it is *basanizō*, which first meant to "examine by torture" and then "torture" or "torment" (cf. NASB, NIV).

Uncleanness (2:10)

Here we have the noun *miasmos* (only here in NT). It comes from the verb *miainō* (four times in NT), which meant to "stain" or "defile."

Government (2:10)

The Greek word is *kyriotēs*, "lordship." Here it probably means "authority" (NASB, NIV).

Presumptuous (2:10)

This is the plural of *tolmētēs* (only here in NT). It comes from the verb *tolmaō*, which means "dare" or "be bold." So it may be translated "daring" (NASB) or "bold" (NIV).

Self-willed (2:10)

For *authadēs* see the discussion at Titus 1:7, first item (WM, 5:260). It has the force of "arrogant" (NIV). Derived from *autos*, "self," and the verb *hēdomai*, "have pleasure," it may well be translated "self-pleasing."

Dignities (2:10)

The Greek has the plural of *doxa,* "glory." This is translated "the glorious ones" (RSV), "angelic majesties" (NASB), and "celestial beings" (NIV). Some commentators refer it to bad angels, some to good angels, and others to angels in general. We simply cannot be certain about the interpretation of this verse.

Natural (2:12)

The adjective *physicos* (only here and Rom. 1:26, 27) is from *physis,* "nature." Mayor (p. 130) translates the phrase here: "born creatures of instinct" (cf. NASB).

Brute (2:12)

The adjective *alogos* (in NT only here; Acts 25:27; and Jude 10) is composed of *a*-negative and *logos,* "reason." So it means "without reason," or "unreasoning" (NASB). The NIV has returned to "brute," which puts it bluntly.

Perish in Their Own Corruption (2:12)

The verb *phtheirō* (fut. pass. here) and the noun *phthora* (based on it) are from the same root and should be translated alike. This is well done in the NASB: "will in the destruction of those creatures also be destroyed."

Feast (2:13)

This is the verb *syneuōcheō* (only here and Jude 12). In the passive, as in both places, it means "feast together with."

That Cannot Cease (2:14)

The adjective *akatapaustos* (only here in NT) is composed of *a*-negative and the compound (intensive) verb *katapauō*. Probably the best translation is "that never cease" (NASB).

Beguiling (2:14)

The verb *deleazō* is found (in NT) only here, in verse 18—where it is translated "allure"—and James 1:14 (see discussion there). It may be translated here "enticing" (NASB) or "seduce" (NIV).

Unstable (2:14)

The adjective *astēriktos* (only here and 3:16) is compounded of *a*-negative and the verb *stērizō*, "fix firmly" or "establish." So it means "unstable" or "unsettled."

Exercised (2:14)

This translation catches the literal meaning here. We find the perfect passive participle of the verb *gymnazō*, for which see the discussion at 1 Tim. 4:8 (WM, 5:201).

That Were Clean Escaped (2:18)

This sounds as if they had completely escaped. The NASB has "who barely escape" and the NIV reads "who are just escaping." Why the difference?

The KJV translation is based on *ontōs*, "being" escaped, found in Aleph (fourth cent.), C (fifth cent.), and many late manuscripts. But Papyrus 72 (third cent.), B (fourth cent.), A (fifth cent.), and the early versions have the adverb *oligōs* (only here in NT), which comes from the adjective *oligos*, "little." So the adverb means "scarcely, barely." This seems to be the better reading.

Pollutions (2:20)

Here we have the plural of the noun *miasma* (only here in NT), which is equivalent to *miasmos* (see discussion of "uncleanness" at verse 10). *Miasma* has been taken over into English with the meaning "poisonous atmosphere"—which we call air "pollution."

Epistle (3:1, 16)

The Greek word *epistolē* occurs 24 times in the NT. In the KJV it is translated "epistle" 15 times and "letter" 9 times (regularly "letter" in NIV). It comes from the verb *epistellō*, "send a message" (especially by writing). So the noun *epistolē* meant what was transmitted, and so a "letter."

Pure (3:1)

The two main Greek adjectives for "pure" are *hagnos* (8 times) and *katharos* (28 times). Here we have *eilikrinēs* (only here and Phil. 1:10). Thayer notes that this word is "commonly supposed to be from *heile* ... sunlight, and *krinō* ["judge"], properly found pure when unfolded and examined by the sun's light" (p. 175). But Trench (p. 319) favors a different etymology and writes: "It is not so much the clear, the transparent, as the purged, the winnowed, the unmingled." He thinks that the best English rendering is "sincere" (cf. NASB).

Minds (3:1)

The Greek word here is not *nous*, but the compound *dianoia*, which basically means "thought" or "understanding." So the NIV has the combination: "wholesome thinking."

Remembrance (3:1)

Hypomnēsis (only here and 2 Tim. 1:5) is best translated "reminder" (NASB; cf. NIV). It is related to the verb "be mindful" *(mimneskō)* in verse 2.

Scoffers (3:3)

This one word (KJV) represents three words in Greek: *en empaigmonē empaiktai*—literally, "in mocking, mockers." Both nouns come from the verb *empaizō,* "mock" (common in the Gospels for the religious leaders mocking Jesus). The first noun is found only here in the NT; the second occurs also in Jude 18. The combination is well represented by "mockers ... with their mocking" (NASB) or "scoffers ... scoffing" (NIV).

Willingly Are Ignorant Of (3:5, 8)

The verb *lanthanō* means "escape notice" (cf. NASB) or "be hidden from." "Deliberately forget" (v. 5) and "forget" (v. 8) in NIV probably catches the thought correctly.

Overflowed (3:6)

This is the aorist passive participle of *kataclyzō* (only here in NT). See discussion at 2:5.

Is . . . Slack . . . Slackness (3:9)

The verb is *bradynō,* "be slow" (only here and 1 Tim. 3:15). The noun is *bradytēs* (only here in NT). Both come from *bradys,* "slow." So the best translation is "be slow" and "slowness" (NASB, NIV).

With a Great Noise (3:10)

This is one word in Greek, *hroizēdon* (only here in NT).

It is onomatopoetic. A. T. Robertson says that it means a "whizzing sound of rapid motion through the air like the flight of a bird, thunder, fierce flame" (WP, 6:176).

Shall Be Burned Up (3:10)

The NIV has "will be laid bare." This, again, is a textual problem. Our oldest Greek manuscripts give three different readings here, and we cannot be absolutely certain as to which is original. But, again, the meaning is much the same.

Conversation (3:11)

See discussion at 1 Pet. 1:15.

Stedfastness (3:17)

The noun is *stērigmos* (only here in NT). It comes from the verb *stērizō*, which, as we have noted before, means "make firm or secure" (cf. "secure position," NIV).

1 JOHN

❧❦❧

Looked Upon (1:1)

"Seen" is the common verb *horaō,* which means "catch sight of." But "looked upon" is the Greek verb *theaomai.* Abbott-Smith gives this definition: *"to behold, look upon, contemplate, view* (in early writers with a sense of *wondering*), in NT of 'careful and deliberate vision which interprets . . . its object'" (p. 203). John the beloved apostle, the author of this Epistle, not only caught sight of Christ but also, over a period of three years, carefully watched Jesus and came to understand who and what He was, the Eternal Logos. And he had actually "touched" Jesus with his own hands. Christ was no phantom; He was real!

Word (1:1)

For the significance of the term *logos,* see discussion at John 1:1 (WM, 2:11-12).

Shew (1:2)

The verb *apangellō* means "to report, announce, declare," which is something stronger than "shew." Arndt and

Gingrich give for this passage "proclaim" (NASB, NIV). In verse 3 the KJV gives the more adequate translation "declare" for this same verb.

Fellowship (1:3)

The Greek word *koinōnia* occurs four times in this chapter (twice in v. 3 and once each in vv. 6 and 7). It is one of the key words of this Epistle.

It comes from the adjective "common" and so means having something in common. That is what fellowship is. It is a sharing. As Hauck observes, "It expresses a two-sided relationship" (TDNT, 3:798). See further discussion at Gal. 2:9 (WM, 4:185).

Message . . . Declare (1:5)

The noun is *angelia* (in NT only here and 3:11). The verb is the compound *anangellō*, which originally meant "bring back word, report," but then was used as equivalent to *apangellō* (see above), "announce" (NASB) or "declare" (NIV).

All (1:7)

This was originally translated "every" in the NIV. It is true that the adjective *pasēs* means both "all" and "every." But to be consistent with verse 9 (same word in Greek), "every" was officially changed to "all" in verse 7, as appears in later printings of the NIV. This is definitely preferable.

Advocate (2:1)

The Greek word is *paraclētos,* for which see discussion at John 14:16 (WM, 2:48-50). In the Gospel the term is used for the Holy Spirit. But here it refers to Christ, and the meaning is clearly that He is our "Advocate" (NASB) or defense lawyer in the court of heaven. The NIV spells it out: "one who speaks to the Father in our defense." All this translates the one word *paraclēton* (accus.).

Propitiation (2:2)

The Greek term *hilasmos* (only here and 4:10) comes from the verb *hilaskomai,* which means "propitiate" or "conciliate"—see discussion at Heb. 2:17 and also of *hilastērion* at Rom. 3:25 (WM, 3:80-83). Since "propitiation" is a technical theological term, not understood by all, the NIV has "atoning sacrifice."

Perfected (2:5)

The Greek verb *teleioō* comes from the adjective *teleios,* "having reached its end" *(telos),* and so "complete" or "perfect." Here we may use "perfected" (KJV, NASB) or "made complete" (NIV).

Pride (2:16)

Alazoneia (only here and James 4:16) basically means "boastfulness." It may well be translated "boastful pride" (NASB; cf. NIV).

Antichrist (2:18, 22; 4:3)

The English term is practically a transliteration of the Greek *antichristos* (only here, four times; and 2 John 7). John uses it to describe anyone who denies the deity (v. 22) or the humanity (4:3; 2 John 7) of Jesus Christ. The latter was denied by the Docetic Gnostics of John's day. They said that Jesus only *seemed* to have a physical body. Following the lead of some Early Church fathers, we have applied the term *antichrist* to the beast of Revelation.

Unction (2:20, 27)

The Greek word is *chrisma* (only here in NT). It comes from *chriō*, "anoint" (with oil), and so means "anointing" (NASB, NIV). The reference is to the Christian being anointed with the Holy Spirit, symbolized by olive oil.

Ye Know All Things (2:20)

This translation is based on the reading *panta* (neut. pl. accus.), found in many manuscripts. But our two fourth-century manuscripts have *pantes* (nom. pl. masc.). This would make the passage read: "you all know" (NASB; cf. NIV)—that is, the truth (v. 21). It is not true that any Christian knows all things. If the reading of the bulk of later manuscripts is correct, "all things" would have to be taken as meaning all things necessary to salvation (v. 27). But it is probably better to accept *pantes* as original—"you all know."

2:23 (italics)

The second half of this verse is in italics in the KJV, which normally indicates that it is not in the Greek. But here the part in italics *is* found in the bulk of the manuscripts and early versions. So it is represented in modern versions with no marginal note.

Abide . . . Remain . . . Continue (2:24)

The translators of the KJV sought for "elegant variation." Here is a good example. The Greek has the same verb, *menō*, in all three places. It is consistently translated "abide(s)" all three times in the NASB. The NIV uses "remain(s)."

Seduce (2:26)

Planaō means "lead astray" or "deceive." We have here the present participle of continuing action. The next verse seems to indicate that these seducers were not succeeding. So the correct meaning is "trying to deceive you" (NASB) or "trying to lead you astray" (NIV).

The Sons of God (3:1-2)

Two things need to be said about this translation (KJV). The first is that the Greek word is not *whioi,* "sons," but *tekna,* "children." The second is that there is no article in the Greek text; it is simply "children of God" (NASB, NIV). When the article is missing in the Greek, it emphasizes kind or quality. We will be called "children of God" because we live godly lives.

A quick comparison will show that recent versions have an added statement in the middle of verse 1—"and such we are" (NASB); "And that is what we are!" (NIV). This is because all the early manuscripts and versions (before the ninth cent.) have *kai esmen,* "and we are." This is a beautiful touch, and it is undoubtedly genuine.

The Transgression of the Law (3:4)

The Greek simply has *hē anomia. Hē* is the definite article (fem.), but while the Greek usually puts the definite article with an abstract noun—it is here used also with "sin"—we normally leave it out in English. Furthermore, *anomia* is from *a*-negative and *nomos,* "law." So the correct translation here is "sin is lawlessness" (NASB, NIV). This is one of the biblical definitions of sin.

Sinneth . . . Sinneth (3:6)

The verb *hamartanō* in both cases is in the present tense of continuing action. This is brought out helpfully by "keeps on sinning . . . continues to sin" (NIV). The one who lives in Christ does not keep on sinning.

This same use of the present tense is found in verse 9. Here again it should be brought out: "No one who is born of God will continue to sin . . . he cannot go on sinning" (NIV).

Good (3:17)

The Greek word is *bios*. Here it indicates "means of subsistence." We do not call that "good" but "goods." So the correct translation here is "the world's goods" (NASB) or "material possessions" (NIV). Trench says that here *bios* indicates "the means of life" or "living" (*Synonyms of the NT*, 91).

This is the last of 10 times that *bios* occurs in the NT (in 1 John only here and 2:16). There it means "life" as lived on earth, "the course of life." Here it means "livelihood."

Bowels (3:17)

See discussion at Phil. 1:8 (WM, 5:15-16).

Try (4:1)

The verb *dokimazō* occurs 23 times in the NT. In the KJV it is translated "prove" most often (10 times) and "try" (4 times). For various meanings of this verb, see the discussion of "prove" at Rom. 12:2 (WM, 3:216). Here the best translation is "test" (RSV, NASB, NIV).

Antichrist (4:3)

See discussion at 2:18.

Only Begotten (4:9)

The Greek word is *monogenēs*. It is compounded of *monos*, "only," and *genos*, "offspring." So it literally means "only begotten."

It is interesting to note in the first three of nine times that *monogenēs* occurs in the NT it is translated in the KJV as "only" (Luke 7:12; 8:42; 9:38). Moreover, in Heb. 11:17 Isaac is said to be the *monogenēs* of Abraham. But Ishmael was also begotten by Abraham! So it is obvious that the main thrust of *monogenēs* is not "only begotten" but "only," perhaps in the sense of "unique." Isaac was unique as the "only" son of promise. In the same way Jesus is *the* "only" Son of God in the sense of full deity. Christians are also called "sons of God," as begotten by the Spirit in the new birth.

Propitiation (4:10)

See discussion at 2:2.

Perfected (4:12)

See discussion at 2:5.

Torment (4:18)

The noun *kolasis* (only here and Matt. 25:46) comes from the verb *kolazō*, "punish." So the literal meaning is "punishment" (NASB, NIV).

Grievous (5:3)

The adjective *barys* is connected with the verb *bareō*,

which means "weigh down." So the adjective means "burdensome" (NASB, NIV). We do not use "grievous" that way today.

Overcometh (5:4, second time)

The Greek participle is in the aorist tense: "has overcome" (NASB, NIV).

Father . . . Word . . . Holy Ghost (5:7)

Anyone who uses a recent scholarly version of the NT will see that these words on the Trinity are not in verse 7. This is because they have no basis in the Greek text. Under Roman Catholic pressure, Erasmus inserted them from the Latin Vulgate. They are not a part of the inspired Bible.

Life (5:11-12)

The noun *zōē* occurs 134 times in the NT. It is translated "life" every time but one (Luke 16:25), where the KJV has "lifetime." The latter idea is usually expressed by *bios* (see discussion at 3:17).

Bultmann begins his treatment of *zōē* by saying: "*Zōē* denotes in Greek the physical vitality of organic beings, animals, men, and also plants. Life is understood, not as a thing, but as vitality, as the nature or manner which characterizes all living creatures as such" (TDNT, 2:832).

In classical Greek *bios* had ethical connotations and *zōē* did not. But when we come to the NT we find the case exactly the reverse. Here we find *bios* used in a material and chronological sense. But *zōē* is the word used, especially by John (36 times in his Gospel and 13 times in his First Epistle), mostly for spiritual life that we have from God in Christ. It is not mere existence, but a new "life."

R. C. Trench puts it very well when he writes:

In revealed religion, which thus makes death to have come into the world through sin, and only through sin, life is the correlative of holiness. Whatever truly lives, does so because sin has never found place in it, or, having found place for a time, has since been overcome and expelled. So soon as ever this is felt and understood, *zōē* at once assumes the profoundest moral significance; it becomes the fittest expression for the very highest blessedness (*Synonyms of the NT,* 95).

Have I Written (5:13)

In view of what we wrote at 5:4, someone might ask why we have "I write" in the NIV. It is true that the verb here is in the aorist tense *(egrapsa)*. But this is what we call the "epistolary aorist." From the point of view of the reader, it would be past time when he got the letter. But for John it was present: "I am writing." In his large *Grammar of the Greek New Testament* (845-46), A. T. Robertson gives a full discussion of this phenomenon, listing 1 John 5:13 as a possible example. However, in his *Word Pictures* (6:25), he says of our passage: "Not epistolary aorist, but refers to verses 1 to 12 of this Epistle." So we can accept either the NASB or NIV on this verse.

Wickedness (5:19)

We do not have here the abstract noun, *ponēria,* but the dative masculine of the adjective *ponēros.* So the correct translation is "the evil one" (NASB, NIV). See a similar situation in Matt. 6:13.

2 JOHN

Elder (v. 1)

The Greek word is *presbyteros*. A. T. Robertson comments: "The word referred originally to age (Luke 15:25), then to rank or office as in the Sanhedrin (Matt. 16:21; Acts 6:12) and in the Christian churches (Acts 11:30; 20:17; I Tim. 5:17, 19) as here also" (WP, 6:249).

Elect Lady (v. 1)

The Greek has *eclectē kyria*. We cannot be certain whether this means a church or an individual.

We . . . We . . . We (v. 8)

The first and third verbs are in the second person plural in all manuscripts earlier than the ninth century. So it is "you" instead of "we."

In the case of the second verb ("wrought"), the first person plural ("we") is found in the fourth-century Vaticanus. For this reason we cannot be certain whether it is "we" (NASB) or "you" (NIV).

Transgresseth (v. 9)

Here we have the present participle of *proagō*—*agō*, "lead," and *pro,* "before." So the verb means "go before, precede, go on ahead." It may be translated here: "goes too far" (NASB) or "runs ahead" (NIV). We are to stay "in step with the Spirit" (Gal. 5:25, NIV).

Doctrine (vv. 9-10)

As we have noted before, the proper translation of *didachē* is "teaching." It comes from the verb *didaskō,* "teach."

Bid Him God Speed (v. 10)

The Greek has *chairein autō . . . legete*—literally "say a greeting to him" (cf. NASB).

Is Partaker Of (v. 11)

This is one word in Greek, *koinōnei*—"shares in" (NIV) or "participates in" (NASB).

Paper (v. 12)

The Greek *chartēs* (only here in NT) was a sheet of "paper," made of papyrus strips.

Ink (v. 12)

Melan (only here; 3 John 13; and 2 Cor. 3:3) literally means "black." It is used in these three places for "ink."

3 JOHN

❦

Wish (v. 2)

The Greek verb is *euchomai,* which means "pray" (NASB, NIV).

Prosper (v. 2)

The verb *euodoō* (in NT only here [twice]; Rom. 1:10; and 1 Cor. 16:2) is compounded of *eu,* "well," and *hodos,* "way." So it originally meant to "have a prosperous journey." Then it was used metaphorically for "prosper."

Be in Health (v. 2)

The Greek has one word, *hygiainein,* from which we get *hygiene.* It means "be sound, healthy, in good health."

After a Godly Sort (v. 6)

The Greek has *axiōs tou theou,* "worthily of God." The NASB and NIV both say: "You will do well to send them on their way in a manner worthy of God." That puts it well.

Receive (v. 8)

The verb is *hypolambanō*. It first meant *"to take* or *bear up"* (by supporting from beneath), and then *"to receive, welcome, entertain"* (A-S, 461). So we could say "support" (NASB) or "show hospitality" (NIV).

Loveth to Have the Preeminence (v. 9)

This is all one word in Greek, the present participle of *philoprōteuō* (only here in NT). The verb is compounded of *phil* (a stem for "love") and *prōtos,* "first." It means "who loves to be first" (NASB, NIV).

Prating Against Us (v. 10)

The verb *phlyareō* is found only here in the NT. A. T. Robertson says it means "to accuse idly and so falsely" (WP, 6:264).

Content (v. 10)

The verb *arkeō* in the passive (as here) means to be "satisfied" (NASB, NIV).

Follow (v. 11)

The verb is *mimeomai,* from which we get *mimic* (found only here; 2 Thess. 3:7, 9; and Heb. 13:7). It means "imitate" (NASB, NIV).

Hath Good Report (v. 12)

This is the perfect passive indicative of the verb *martyreō,* "witness." In late Greek it came to have the meaning in the passive: "to have a good report, to be approved." It means that "Demetrius is well spoken of by everyone" (NIV).

Record (v. 12)

"Bear record" is the same verb, *martyreō*, "witness" or "testify." The second "record" is the noun *martyria*, "witness" (NASB) or "testimony" (NIV).

Pen (v. 13)

The Greek noun is *kalamos*. It basically meant "a reed." In the NT the word is used for a "stalk" or "staff" and for a "measuring rod" in Revelation (11:21; 21:15 f.). Here alone (in NT) it is used for a "pen."

For "ink" see note at 2 John 12.

JUDE

❧⟐❧

Sanctified (v. 1)

Again we have a textual problem. Is it "sanctified" (KJV) or "loved" (NIV; cf. NASB). The facts are that *hēgiasmenois*, "sanctified," is not found in any Greek manuscript before the ninth century. Papyrus 72 (third cent.), Aleph and B (fourth cent.), A (fifth cent.), Psi (eighth cent.), many minuscules, and the oldest versions all have here *ēgapēmenois*, perfect passive participle of the well-known verb *agapaō*, "love."

Earnestly Contend (v. 3)

This is one word in Greek, the present infinitive of the strong compound verb (hence, "earnestly") *epagōnizomai* (only here in NT). The simple verb *agonizomai* first meant to compete in an athletic contest, and then, more generally, to "fight, struggle, strive." We are to be earnest in our defense of the faith.

Crept In Unawares (v. 4)

This is one word in Greek, the second aorist passive

indicative of *pareisdyō* (only here in NT). It is compounded of *para*, "beside," *eis*, "in," and *dyō*, "plunge." So it means to slip in secretly (cf. NIV), as if by a side door.

Put You in Remembrance (v. 5)

We would say, "remind you" (NASB, NIV). See discussion at 2 Pet. 1:12.

First Estate (v. 6)

The Greek single word is *archē*. The term literally means "beginning" or "rule." Here it probably means "domain" (NASB) or "positions of authority" (NIV). Jude is discussing the fallen angels.

Giving Themselves Over to Fornication (v. 7)

This is all one word in Greek, the aorist participle of *ekporneuō* (only here in NT). As we have noted before, the noun *porneia*, which is always translated "fornication" (26 times) in the KJV, takes in more than that term indicates today. It includes all "sexual immorality" (NIV) or "gross immorality" (NASB). This is further enlarged here by the additional "going after strange flesh," which rather obviously suggests homosexuality.

Dignities (v. 8)

See discussion at 2 Pet. 2:10.

A Railing Accusation (v. 9)

The Greek has *krisin . . . blasphēmias*. The noun *blasphēmia* (here in the genitive) first meant "slander," and then, as applied to speaking against God, "blasphemy." *Krisis* (accus. here) means "judgment" (cf. NASB). But the context here suggests for the whole expression: "a slanderous accusation" (NIV).

Brute (v. 10)

See discussion at 2 Pet. 2:12.

Gainsaying (v. 11)

Antilogia (in NT only here and Heb. 6:16; 7:7; 12:3) literally means "a speaking against" *(anti)*. In the papyri it has the meaning "strife." Here it has its strongest meaning, "rebellion" (NASB, NIV).

Spots (v. 12)

The word is the plural of *spilas*. In the classics it was used for "a *rock* or reef over which the sea dashes" (A-S, 414). This meaning was adopted in the NASB. But Abbott-Smith goes on to note that in later writers it was equated with *spilos,* "spot" or "stain." Both meanings make good sense in this passage, taking the term, in either case, as metaphorical.

Convince (v. 15)

As we have noted before, the verb *elengchō* should be translated "convict" (NASB, NIV).

Murmurers (v. 16)

The noun *gongystēs* (only here in NT) is onomatopoetic. It is best translated "grumblers" (NASB, NIV).

Complainers (v. 16)

Mempsimoiros (only here in NT) is an adjective (pl.

here), meaning "complaining of one's fate." It may also be translated "finding fault" (NASB) or "faultfinders" (NIV).

Great Swelling Words (v. 16)

This is all one word in Greek, the neuter plural of the adjective *hyperonkos* (only here and 2 Pet. 2:18). The adjective means "excessive, immoderate" and was used in later writers for arrogant speech (cf. NASB).

Having Men's Persons in Admiration (v. 16)

This is two words in Greek: *thaumazontes prosōpa*—literally, "admiring faces." It means "flattering people" (NASB; cf. NIV).

Because of Advantage (v. 16)

The Greek is: *epheleias charin. Epheleia* (only here and Rom. 3:1) means "profit" or "advantage." *Charin* means "for the sake of" (cf. NASB, NIV).

They Who Separate Themselves (v. 19)

The Greek has the plural definite article *hoi* and the present participle of the double compound verb *apodiorizō* (only here in NT). It is based on *horos*, "boundary," *dia*, "through," and *apo*, "away from"—to mark off boundaries. Here it is used metaphorically in the sense of "make separations." The reference is to people "who cause divisions" (NASB).

Making a Difference (v. 22)

The Greek has the plural of the present middle participle of *diakrinō* in the accusative case, which means "doubting." It seems that the true meaning here is "who are doubting" (NASB) or "those who doubt" (NIV).

REVELATION

❧❀❦

Revelation (1:1)

The very first word of this last book of the Bible is *apocalypsis.* That is why we often refer to this book as "the Apocalypse."

The Greek term literally means "an uncovering"—see discussion at Gal. 1:12 (WM, 4:177-79). That is what we have in the Book of Revelation: an uncovering of the unknown future, what could not at all be known except by a divine revelation.

Signified (1:1)

The Greek verb is *sēmainō* (in the aorist), which comes from *sēma,* "a sign." So it means "to give a sign, signify, indicate" (A-S, 405), or "make known, report, communicate" (AG, 755). Lange says of it here: "*Esēmanen* is a modification of *deixai* [show], indicative of the signs employed, the symbolical representation" (*Commentary on the Holy Scriptures,* Revelation, 89).

Rengstorf thinks that the verb, as used here, only means "to indicate or declare something" (TDNT, 7:264).

But he does note that Philo (first cent.) used it with the connotation: "this means (in the deeper sense)" (p. 265).

In spite of objections, we do feel that there may be some "significance"—pardon the play on words!—in John's use of *sēmainō* here. He uses the verb three times in his Gospel (12:33; 18:32; 21:19) with what might be called prophetic significance.

In support of our position on its use in Rev. 1:1 we note that Bengel says that "the LXX use *sēmainein* to express a great sign of a great thing: Ezek. xxxiii.3" (*Gnomon of the NT,* 5:185). Vincent observes, "The word is appropriate to the symbolical character of the revelation, and so in John xii.33, where Christ predicts the mode of his death in a figure" (WS, 2:408). The first meaning given for *sēmainō* in the famous Liddell-Scott *Lexicon* is: "show by a sign, indicate, point out" (p. 1592). And Edward McDowell writes, "The author implies that the message he has received is being given to his readers under signs or symbols. Attention to this fact should save us from crass literalism in interpreting the message of the book" (p. 24).

Someone has suggested that if we pronounce "signified" as *"sign-*ified" we would get the right idea. Perhaps so.

Asia (1:4)

In the NT the term "Asia" never means the continent, as it does for us today. Rather it is "the province of Asia" (NIV), the western part of Asia Minor (modern Turkey).

The Seven Spirits (1:4)

The reference is to the Holy Spirit in all His perfection (the number "seven"). It is the one Holy Spirit manifesting himself and ministering to the seven churches (v. 4).

Prince (1:5)

Archōn is better translated "ruler" (NASB, NIV).

Washed (1:5)

This translates *lousanti*, from the verb *louo*, "bathe." But all the manuscripts earlier than the ninth century have *lusanti*, from *luo*, "loose." So the correct translation is "released" (NASB) or "freed" (NIV).

Kings (1:6)

The Greek has *basileian*, which means "a kingdom" (NASB, NIV). Of course, the sense is much the same.

Alpha . . . Omega (1:8)

These are the first and last letters of the Greek alphabet. So it means "the beginning and the ending" (KJV). But these explanatory words are not in A and C (fifth cent.), though they are in Sinaiticus (fourth cent.)—Vaticanus (fourth cent.) ends at Heb. 9:14. Since the external evidence (manuscripts) is rather evenly balanced, this case has to be settled by internal evidence. Bruce Metzger puts it well: "If the longer text were original no good reason can be found to account for the shorter text, whereas the presence of the longer expression in 21:6 obviously prompted some copyists to expand the text here" (*Textual Commentary on the Greek NT,* 732). Again we would note that the meaning of the passage is not affected by this.

Companion (1:9)

Sygkoinōnos (sometimes spelled *synkoinōnos*) is compounded of *syn,* "together," and the adjective *koinos,* "common." So it means a "sharer, partaker, participant."

Patience of Jesus Christ (1:9)

This translation obviously does not make sense in this passage. The Greek says: *hypomonē en Iēsou. En* means "in." We have noted a number of times that *hypomonē* does not mean "patience" but "endurance" or "perseverance." We have this "in Jesus" (NASB, NIV).

For (1:9)

This (KJV) would suggest that John was on Patmos to preach the gospel. But the Greek has *dia* with the accusative, which means "because of" (NASB, NIV). John was there as a political prisoner of the Roman Empire because of his preaching.

The Lord's Day (1:10)

Some have assumed that this means "the day of the Lord," found often in Scripture. But here "Lord's" is an adjective, *kyriakē,* found only here and in 1 Cor. 11:20—"the Lord's supper." In modern Greek, Sunday is called *Kyriakē.* R. H. Charles says of this passage in Revelation: "Here 'Lord's Day' has become a technical designation of Sunday" (ICC, Revelation, 1:23). Why Sunday? Foerster writes, "The Lord's Day takes its significance from the resurrection of Christ" (TDNT, 3:1096). Jesus was in the grave on Saturday, the Jewish Sabbath. On Sunday we worship the risen Lord!

I Am . . . the Last (1:11)

All of this is absent in the early manuscripts (before the ninth cent.). It was added by a later copyist. The same is true of "which are in Asia."

Book (1:11)

The Greek word is *biblion,* from which we get our word "Bible." The reference is to a papyrus "scroll" (NIV), which would be less expensive than parchment (animal skins). The scroll of Revelation would be about 15 feet long.

Candlesticks (1:13)

The Greek *lychnias* means "lampstands" (NASB, NIV). See discussion at Matt. 5:15 (WM, 1:19).

Girt About the Paps . . . Girdle (1:13)

How much more beautiful is the NIV: "with a golden sash around his chest."

Brass (1:15)

Chalkolibanon (in NT only here and 2:18) is a word not found elsewhere in literature, except in reference to these passages. So we are not sure of the exact meaning. But "bronze" or "burnished bronze" (RSV, NASB) seems the nearest we can get to it.

Hell (1:18)

The Greek should be transliterated "Hades" (NASB, NIV), the place of departed spirits. "Hell" is the Greek *Gehenna* (not used here).

Angels (1:20)

The Greek word *angelos* means "messenger" and is used for human messengers in Luke 7:24; 9:52; and James 2:25. It is true that in the 60 or more times that *angelos* occurs in the Book of Revelation it refers to "angels." But we feel that here it may *possibly* mean the pastors of the seven churches. However, George E. Ladd concludes his study of the term here by saying: "It is best to understand this as a rather unusual symbol to represent the heavenly or supernatural character of the church" (p. 35).

Patience (2:2)

Should be "perseverance" (NASB, NIV). See my commentary on Revelation (BBC, 10:492).

Tried (2:2)

Should be "tested" (NIV; cf. NASB).

Fainted (2:3)

The Greek verb is *kopiaō,* which means "grow weary." Instead of "hast laboured, and hast not fainted" (KJV), the Greek simply has *kai ou kekopiakas*—"and have not grown weary" (NASB, NIV).

Somewhat (2:4)

This added word in italics (KJV) gives entirely the wrong meaning to this verse. It is not "somewhat"—some *little* thing that has gone wrong. The Greek very clearly says: "But I have against you that you have left your first love." This was not a trifling matter, as verse 5 points out emphatically. They had to "repent" and start all over again!

Nicolaitans (2:6)

In spite of speculation by Irenaeus and some other ancient church fathers, we have no knowledge as to who these heretics were. The term *Nicolaitōn* (pl.) occurs only here and in verse 15.

Overcometh (2:7, 11, 17, 26; 3:5, 12, 21)

The verb *nikaō* comes from the noun *nikē,* "victory." So it literally means to "be a victor." In 1 John 5:4 we find the verb twice and the noun once. (*Nikē* occurs only there in the NT.)

Paradise (2:7)

See discussion at 2 Cor. 12:4 (WM, 4:159).

Works (2:9, 13)

Erga is not found in the better Greek manuscripts (with the exception of Aleph in verse 9 but not in verse 13) and so is not included in good versions. It seems like a scribal echo of verse 2.

Crown (2:10)

See discussion at 1 Cor. 9:25 (WM, 4:61).

Seat (2:13)

The Greek word is *thronos,* from which we get "throne" —the correct translation here (NASB, NIV).

Commit Fornication (2:14, 20)

The verb *porneuō* takes in more than fornication. It includes all "sexual immorality" (NIV).

In (2:17)

The Greek does not have *en,* "in," but *epi,* "upon." The new name was not written "in the stone" (KJV) but "on" it (NASB, NIV).

A Few Things (2:20)

This addition (KJV) has practically no support in the Greek manuscripts.

Space (2:21)

The Greek word *chronos*, from which we get *chronology*, means "time," not "space."

Their (2:22)

The Greek manuscripts give somewhat stronger support to *autēs*, "her" (NASB, NIV), than to *autōn*, "their." Again we would note that a copyist would be more apt to change "her" to "their" than to do the reverse. And once more we would say that the difference in meaning is very slight.

Reins (2:23)

Nephros (only here in NT) literally meant (in pl.) "the kidneys." It is used in the Septuagint for the kidneys of sacrificed animals (Exod. 29:13, etc.). Then it came to be used figuratively for the inward part of man, as in Job 16:13 (TDNT, 4:911).

We have here a loose quotation from Jer. 11:20. *Nephrous* may be translated "minds" (NASB).

Power (2:26)

The Greek word is not *dynamis*, "power," but *exousia*, "authority" (NASB, NIV).

Be Watchful (3:2)

The Greek has the present imperative of the verb *ginomai*, "become," followed by the present participle of *grēgo-*

reō, "to be awake." So a good translation is "Wake up" (NASB, NIV).

Perfect (3:2)

This is not the adjective *teleios,* which is usually translated "perfect" (KJV). Rather, it is the perfect passive participle of *plēroō,* "fill." So it means "filled up," or "complete" (NIV; cf. NASB).

Defiled (3:4)

The verb *molynō* means to "stain" or "soil" (cf. NASB, NIV). Arndt and Gingrich comment here: "Unsoiled garments as symbol of a spotless life" (pp. 526-27).

Spue (3:16)

The verb *emeō* (only here in NT) literally means to "vomit," and so "to reject with extreme disgust" (WP, 6:321).

I Am . . . Increased with Goods (3:17)

This is all one word in Greek, *peploutēka,* the perfect active indicative of *plouteō,* which means "be rich" and is translated that way in verse 18 (KJV). "I am rich" (v. 17, all versions) is *eimi,* "I am," with the adjective *plousios,* "rich." For variation (as in KJV) the verb here could be translated "have become wealthy" (NASB) or "I have acquired wealth" (NIV).

Tried in the Fire (3:18)

This is a striking expression in the Greek: *pepyrōmenon ek pyros. Pyr* is the Greek word for "fire" (used throughout NT). It is preceded here by the perfect passive participle of *pyroō,* "set on fire, burn." Clearly the idea here is "refined by fire" (NASB).

Chasten (3:19)

Paideuō is better translated "discipline" (NASB, NIV). See discussion at Heb. 12:5.

Was Opened (4:1)

This suggests that John saw a door just being opened in heaven. But the Greek is *ēneōgmenē,* the perfect passive participle of *anoigō,* "to open." The perfect tense indicates a continuing state resulting from a completed act. So the correct translation is "standing open" (NASB, NIV).

Spirit (4:2)

The uncial Greek manuscripts (4th to 9th cent.) have all large letters, while the minuscule (cursive) manuscripts (9th to 15th cent.) have all small letters. So the Greek does not indicate whether we should have "in the spirit" (KJV)—in a trance—or "in the Spirit"—in the control of the Holy Spirit. The latter (NASB, NIV) seems preferable. The Holy Spirit was giving John a divine revelation of the future.

Jasper . . . Sardine (4:3)

The Greek word *iaspis* occurs only here and three times in chapter 21 (vv. 11, 18, 19). Abbott-Smith says of it: "apparently not the modern stone of that name, but a translucent stone" (p. 212). *Sardion* (only here and 21:20) is defined by Abbott-Smith as "the *sardian* stone, *sard* (of which *carnelian* is one variety)" (p. 402). The KJV has "sardine" because the late manuscripts have *sardinos.* Pliny says that the stone was named after the city of Sardis (3:1).

A third item is mentioned here, a "rainbow." The Greek word is *iris* (only here and 10:1), given as a name to the iris plant.

This rainbow is often connected with the "rainbow" of promise after the Flood. But the Greek word there in the Septuagint (Gen. 9:13, 14, 16) is *toxon.* H. B. Swete sounds this note of warning: "Since *iris* is substituted for *toxon,* it is precarious to press a reference to the rainbow of the covenant" (p. 68).

Thunderings (4:5)

The Greek word is the plural of *phōnē,* which means "sound, tone, noise," and then "voice" (AG, 870). Here it probably means "sounds" (NASB) or "rumblings" (NIV).

Voices (4:5)

The Greek word is *brontē* (in Revelation 10 out of 12 times in NT), which means "thunder." Since it is in the plural here, it may be translated "peals of thunder" (NASB, NIV).

Beasts (4:6)

Here we have the plural of *zōon,* which occurs in Heb. 13:11; 2 Pet. 2:12; Jude 10; and 20 times in Revelation. It is always translated "beast" in the KJV. This is unfortunate, for today "beast" is used mostly for a wild animal or a brutal person. These here were heavenly beings, literally "living creatures" (NASB, NIV)—from *zōē,* "life." The real "beast" of Revelation is indicated by the Greek word *thērion,* "wild beast," which occurs 38 times in this book and is correctly translated "beast."

Calf (4:7)

The word is *moschos*. A. T. Robertson says of it: *"Moschos* is first a sprout, then the young of animals, then a calf (bullock or heifer) as in Luke 15:23, 27, 30, or a full-grown ox (Ezek. 1:10)" (WP, 6:329).

O Lord (4:11)

The Greek text has *ho kyrios kai ho theos hēmōn,* "our Lord and God" (NIV; cf. NASB).

For Thy Pleasure (4:11)

The Greek says *dia to thelēma sou* — literally, "because of Thy will" (NASB), and so, "by your will" (NIV). In a 10-page discussion of *thelēma* (TDNT, 3:52-62), Schrenk shows clearly that *thelēma* means "will."

They Are and Were Created (4:11)

The Greek has *ēsan kai ektisthēsan* — literally, "they were and were created." This is a bit difficult to translate into meaningful English. Swete gives this helpful interpretation: "The Divine Will had made the universe a fact in the scheme of things before the Divine Power gave material expression to the fact" (p. 75).

Book (5:1, etc.)

When we say "book" today we mean a bound volume. But that is not what we have here. Schrenk writes: "The *biblion* with seven seals (5:1-5, 7f) is again in the form of a roll ... not a codex" (TDNT, 1:618). "Codex" is the technical name for a bound book, such as we find from the fourth century on, but not in the first century. So it is better to say "scroll" (NIV).

Loose (5:2)

That is the basic meaning of *luō*. But with "seals" it means "break" (NASB, NIV). When the seals were broken, then it would be possible to "open the scroll" (vv. 2, 3, 4, 5, NIV).

Prevailed (5:5)

The verb is *nikaō*, which comes from the noun *nikē*, "victory." So a better translation is "overcome" (NASB) or "triumphed" (NIV). Swete comments:

> The Lion of Judah, the Son of David, conquered the world (Jo. xvi.33 . . .), and one fruit of His victory is that it belongs to Him to open the seals of God's Book of Destiny, i.e. to carry history onward through successive stages to the final revelation *(p. 77)*.

Root (5:5)

The basic meaning of the noun *hriza* is "root." But scholars are agreed that here it means the "shoot" that comes out of the root. For instance, Maurer contends that here *hriza* must be translated "shoot (out) of David"—genitive of origin (TDNT, 6:989). So "Root of David" is basically equivalent to the familiar "Son of David."

Lamb (5:6, 8, 12, 13)

Outside the Book of Revelation the Greek noun *arnion* occurs only in John 21:15, where it is used (pl.) for young believers. It is a diminutive form of *arnē*.

In Isa. 53:7 the word for "lamb" in the Septuagint is *amnos*. Swete writes:

> *Amnos* has passed from the LXX into the other passages in the N.T. where Christ is described as the Lamb (Jo. i.29, 36, Acts viii.32, 1 Pet. i.19), but it does

not occur in the Apocalypse, which uses *to arnion* as a
title of our Lord 29 times in 12 chapters *(p. 78).*

Swete goes on to say:

> The diminutive must not be pressed, ... but the
> contrast of the Lamb with the Lion is sufficiently strik-
> ing in any case, directing attention to the unique combi-
> nation of majesty and meekness which characterized the
> life of Jesus Christ *(ibid.).*

Odours (5:8)

The word *odor* is generally used today for a bad smell.
Unfortunately, the KJV uses it here and in 18:13 for the
noun *thymiama* (in the pl.), which means "incense" (NASB,
NIV). For some unknown reason, in 8:3 and 4 it is correctly
translated "incense" in the KJV.

Redeemed (5:9)

The verb is *agorazō,* which comes from *agora,* "market-
place." So it meant "to buy in the market, purchase" (A-S,
7). In fact, in the KJV it is translated "buy" in 28 of the 31
times it occurs in the NT. Only here and in 14:3 and 4 is it
"redeemed." Christ actually "purchased" (NIV) us with His
own blood.

Kindred (5:9)

The Greek word *phylē* means "tribe" (NASB, NIV). It
refers over a dozen times to the tribes of Israel. But in Matt.
24:30 and half a dozen times in Revelation it is used for the
tribes of the earth. "Tongue," of course, means "language"
(NIV). With Christ there is no distinction of race, language,
or nationality.

Come and See (6:1, 3, 5, 7)

Why do all scholarly versions today omit "and see"?

The simple fact is that, with the exception of Aleph (4th cent.), no Greek manuscript earlier than the 10th century has these words. It seems clear that they were not a part of the original text.

"Come and see" (KJV) would be a call to John to come and see what was about to happen. But "Come" was probably a summons to each of the four horsemen to ride out into view. The modern parallel would be a trumpet blast that called a rider on horseback to burst out into the arena in front of the spectators. (For interpretation of the four riders see BBC, 10:540-43.)

A Pair of Balances (6:5)

This is one word in Greek, *zygon*, which literally means "a yoke" and is so translated the other five times it occurs in the NT (Matt. 11:29, 30; Acts 15:10; Gal. 5:1; 1 Tim. 6:1). It is used there metaphorically in the sense of submission to authority. But here it is used, as in the Septuagint of Isaiah 40:12, for "a pair of scales" (NASB, NIV). Here it suggests a great shortage of food (v. 6). Rengstorf notes: "Models for the use of scales as a symbol of dearth are perhaps to be found in Lv. 26:26; Ez. 4:16, though the word *zygos* is not used in these passages" (TDNT, 2:898).

Measure (6:6)

This term is very indefinite. The Greek word *choinix* (only here in NT) indicated a dry measure equivalent to about a "quart" (NASB, NIV).

Penny (6:6)

The Greek word is *dēnarion*. Occurring 16 times in the NT, it is translated (KJV) 9 times as "penny," 5 times as "pence," and twice as "pennyworth." But this is misleading.

The Roman "denarius" (Latin form) was a silver coin worth about 18 cents. Furthermore, it represented a day's wages (Matt. 20:2). In the famine predicted here, a person would have to spend a day's wages just to buy a quart of wheat or three quarts of barley (the food of the poor people). The correct rendering is "denarius" (RSV, NASB) or "day's wages" (NIV)—to represent the enormity of the price.

Pale (6:8)

The Greek adjective is *chlōros.* It literally means "green" (Mark 6:39; Rev. 8:7). But it was used by Hippocrates and others for *"pale* as the color of a person in sickness as contrasted with his appearance in health" (AG, 882). That is its meaning here.

Death (6:8)

The Greek has *thanatos,* the common word for death (117 times in NT). Why, then, is it here translated "pestilence" (RSV, NASB) and "plague" (NIV)?

The answer is that *thanatos* often means "pestilence" in the Septuagint. Also, there is a close parallel here with Ezek. 14:21, which reads: "How much more when I send my four sore judgments upon Jerusalem, the sword, and the famine, and the noisome beast, and the pestilence." The same four things are mentioned, with the last two in reverse order.

Untimely Figs (6:13)

This is one word in Greek, *olynthous* (only here in NT). *Olynthos* (sing.) is defined by Abbott-Smith as meaning *"an unripe fig,* which grows in winter and usually falls off in the spring" (p. 316). So it may be translated "unripe figs" (NASB) or "late figs" (NIV).

Departed (6:14)

The verb *apochōrizō* (in NT only here and Acts 15:39) is compound of *apo*, "away from," and *chōrizō*, "divide, separate." So it means "was split apart" (NASB) or "receded" (NIV).

Chief Captains (6:15)

The Greek word is *chiliarchos*, a chiliarch or "commander of a thousand men" (used many times in Acts). The plural can well be translated "commanders" (NASB) or "generals" (NIV). "Captain" is a lower rank today.

Palms (7:9)

Since all human hands have "palms," the KJV "palms in their hands" could be a bit awkward. The Greek word for "palm" is *phoinix*, which means the date-palm tree. This word occurs once elsewhere in the NT (John 12:13). There it is preceded by *baia* (only here in NT), the word for a "palm branch." So the whole expression is translated "branches of palm trees" (KJV). To avoid awkwardness here in Revelation it would be best to say "palm branches" (NASB, NIV).

Great Tribulation (7:14)

The Greek has *tēs thlipseōs tēs megalēs*—literally, "the tribulation, the great"; that is, "the Great Tribulation." The article should be retained in English translation.

Shall Dwell Among Them (7:15)

The Greek says *skēnōsei ep' autous*. The verb *skēnoō* comes from *skēnē*, "tent" or "tabernacle." And the primary meaning of *epi (ep')* is "upon." So the whole expression here may be translated "shall spread His tabernacle over them"

(NASB) or "will spread his tent over them" (NIV). It is a beautiful picture of God's protecting care.

Heat (7:16)

The Greek noun *kauma* (only here and 16:9) comes from the verb *kaiō,* which has the strong meaning of "burn, destroy by fire" in some passages. So the noun may be translated "burning heat" (AG, 425) or "scorching heat" (NIV; also AG in 16:9).

Feed (7:17)

Once more (see discussion at John 21:16 in WM, 2:60) the KJV falls short. The verb here is not *boskō,* "feed," but *poimainō.* The latter comes from the noun *poimēn,* "shepherd." So it means to "shepherd." Hence, the correct translation is "will be their shepherd" (NIV; cf. NASB).

Voices (8:5)

See discussion at 4:5.

Sounded (8:7)

The verb is *salpizō,* which comes from the noun *salpix,* "trumpet." So it means to "sound a trumpet" (used mostly in Revelation). It is not necessary to repeat "trumpets" at the end of verse 6, but perhaps it is well in verse 7 to say "sounded his trumpet" (NIV).

Burnt Up (8:7)

This is the compound verb *katakaiō,* intensive form of *kaiō,* "burn." So it means "burn up" or "burn completely."

This occurs twice in the KJV. But in all scholarly versions there is in front of those two clauses another clause: "A third of the earth was burned up" (cf. RSV, NASB). This clause is found in practically all the early Greek manuscripts of the NT. It almost certainly is genuine. With three consecutive clauses ending the same, and the first two beginning the same, it would be very easy for a copyist to omit one. This is a fairly common mistake made by typists today.

Lamp (8:10)

This is the Greek word *lampas*, which clearly means "lamp" in the parable of the 10 virgins (five times in Matt. 25:1, 3, 4, 7, 8), because fed with oil. They were tiny clay lamps, such as have been excavated from those days. But here the *lampas* was probably a "torch" (NASB, NIV), which is the first meaning for *lampas* given in Greek lexicons.

An Angel (8:13)

The Greek literally says "one eagle," *henos aetou*. So it is properly translated "an eagle" (RSV, NASB, NIV). *Angelos* is found in some late manuscripts and so got into the Textus Receptus. It is easy to see why a later copyist would change *aetos* to *angelos*, as being more natural, but not why anyone would do the reverse. It seems probable, however, that it was an angel who appeared in the form of an eagle for striking effect.

The Bottomless Pit (9:1, 2)

The Greek says "the shaft of the Abyss" (NIV): *to phrear tēs abyssou. Phrear* means "well" (Luke 14:5; John 4:11, 12), and then "shaft." This noun occurs once in verse 1 and three times in verse 2 and is translated "pit" (KJV, NASB). It had this meaning in later Greek.

We get our word *abyss* from *abyssos.* This term occurs in Rom. 10:7 for the abode of the dead—the common Greek usage. In Luke 8:31 it evidently refers to the abode of demons. Then it occurs seven times in Revelation (9:1, 2, 11; 11:7; 17:8; 20:1, 3).

In classical Greek *abyssos* was an adjective meaning "bottomless." Then it came to be used as a substantive, and is best transliterated simply as "Abyss" (NIV). Cremer says that in this sense "it is only used in biblical and ecclesiastical Greek" (p. 2). Joachim Jeremias writes:

> In the NT *abyssos* is thought of as a "prison for spirits" (Rev. 9:1; 20:1, 3). . . . Its inmates until their release in the tribulation before the end are Antichrist (Rev. 11:7; 17:8 . . .), the prince of the underworld (Rev. 9:11), demons (Lk. 8:13) and scorpion centaurs (Rev. 9:3 ff.). After the *parousia* Satan will be shut up in it during the millennial kingdom (20:1, 3) *(TDNT, 1:10).*

Torment (9:5)

This occurs three times in this verse, first as a verb and then twice as a noun. The verb *basanizō* is in the future passive and so is correctly translated in the KJV. The noun is *basanismos.*

The verb properly meant "to rub on a touchstone, put to the test," and then "to examine by torture," and so "to torture, torment" (A-S, 76). The noun, which occurs only in Revelation (9:5; 14:11; 18:7, 10, 15), means "torture" or "torment."

Shall Flee (9:6)

Pheugei is the present indicative of *pheugō,* "flee," and so literally means "flees" (NASB).

Abaddon . . . Apollyon (9:11)

The Hebrew *abaddōn* means "destruction." The Greek

noun *apollyōn* comes from the verb *apollymi,* "destroy," and so means "destruction."

In (9:14)

The Greek preposition is *epi,* "upon." When referring to a vicinity it means "at" or "by." These four angels were not bound "in" the great river but "at" that place (NASB, NIV). "In" would be the Greek *en.*

Loose (9:14)

The verb *luō* does mean "loose." But "release" (NASB, NIV) is the more contemporary term.

Two Hundred Thousand Thousand (9:16)

We would say, "Two hundred million" (NASB, NIV).

Of Fire (9:17)

The Greek has the adjective *pyrinos* (only here in NT), which means "fiery." This obviously refers to color, not content. So it is best rendered "the color of fire" (NASB) or "fiery red."

Of Jacinth (9:17)

The Greek has the adjective *hyakinthinos* (only here in NT), "of hyacinth" (NASB). Swete writes, "Here *hyakinthinos* is doubtless meant to describe the blue smoke of a sulphurous flame" (p. 123). So the NIV simply has "dark blue."

Brimstone (9:17)

The adjective *theiōdēs* (only here in NT) meant "sulphurous." The NIV keeps the color pattern by saying: "yellow as sulphur."

Sorceries (9:21)

The Greek noun *pharmakon,* from which we get *pharmacy,* occurs only here in the NT. It literally meant "a drug," and then "an incantation, enchantment" (A-S, 466). Many manuscripts have the plural of *pharmakeia,* which means "magic arts" (NIV). That is probably what is meant, in either case.

Fornication (9:21)

See discussion at Matt. 5:32 (WM, 1:23).

Time No Longer (10:6)

It is true that the noun is *chronos,* from which we get *chronology,* and that its basic meaning is "time" (in the sense of a period of time). But many Greek writers used it for a "delay," and that seems to be the real meaning here (NASB, NIV). Delling suggests "the 'delay' that is granted to allow time for conversion, Rev. 2:21, or 'postponement' in Rev. 10:6" (TDNT, 9:591). He goes on to say, "Rev. 10:6 does not mean that time itself comes to an end. All that is meant is that the judgment of God will be delayed no longer" (p. 592). That seems clearly to be the meaning here.

Declared (10:7)

The Greek verb is *euangelizō,* which basically means "announce good news." It is almost always in the middle or passive in the NT, as in classical Greek. Only in later writers was it used in the active, as we find it here and in 14:6.

In most of the NT it is people who do the announcing.

But here it is God. Friedrich writes, "In Rev. 10:7 God has revealed His plan of salvation to His servants the prophets of the OT and the NT. It is good news because it proclaims the coming of the Messiah, of the *basileia tou theou,* after the overthrow of the dominion of Antichrist" (TDNT, 2:721). This is "the mystery of God," mentioned in this verse.

Belly (10:9, 10)

In the KJV *koilia* is translated "womb" 12 times and "belly" 11 times. The obvious meaning here is "stomach" (NASB, NIV).

Reed . . . Rod (11:1)

The first word is *kalamos.* It is most naturally translated "reed" in Matt. 11:7; 12:20; but in Matt. 27:29 and 30 as "staff." In 3 John 13 we found it used a third way, for a reed "pen" with which John was writing. Here it is a reed used for a measuring rod (NIV).

The second word is *hrabdos,* which was often used for a "staff" (NASB) on a journey (e.g., Matt. 10:10). But it was also used for a ruler's staff, or "scepter" (Rev. 2:27; 12:5; 19:15).

The various meanings of these two words account for the variety of translations in the different versions. This is true of many Greek words in the NT. Frustrated readers often ask, "Which is correct?" The answer is: "All."

Them That Worship (11:1)

The NIV says, "Count the worshipers." In the Greek there is no word here for "count." But it seems obvious that John was not told to measure the physical height of the worshipers. A. T. Robertson wisely observes: "Perhaps measuring as applied to 'them that worship therein' implies a word like numbering" (WP, 6:376-77).

Temple (11:1)

The Greek word is not *hieron,* the "Temple area" (Mark 11:15), but *naos,* which refers particularly to the sanctuary itself. John was specifically instructed not to measure the "outer court" (v. 2, NIV), which in Jesus' day was called the Court of the Gentiles.

Power (11:3)

As indicated by italics (KJV; "authority," NASB), this is not in the Greek. But it appears to be the proper sense (NIV).

Candlesticks (11:4)

The correct translation of *lychniai* is "lampstands." See discussion at Matt. 5:15 (WM, 1:19).

Will Hurt (11:5)

This sounds like a simple future. But the Greek says *thelei adikēsai,* "desires to harm" (NASB) or "tries to harm" (NIV). The verb *thelō* precedes *adikēsai* both times in this verse. It also occurs at the end of verse 6 (in the future tense).

The Bottomless Pit (11:7)

See discussion at 9:1.

Spiritually (11:8)

The Greek does have the adverb *pneumatikōs* (only here

and 1 Cor. 2:14), which comes from *pneuma,* "spirit," and so literally means "spiritually." But, as A. T. Robertson notes, it here indicates "in a hidden or mystical (allegorical) sense" (WP, 6:381). This is represented well by "mystically" (NASB) or "figuratively" (NIV).

Spirit (11:11)

Pneuma first meant "wind," then "breath," and finally "spirit." It is obvious that the correct translation here is "breath" (NASB, NIV).

Remnant (11:13)

The Greek *loipoi* is from the verb *leipō,* "leave behind." So it means those who were left. We call these "survivors" (NIV).

Kingdoms (11:15)

The Greek is singular, *basileia,* "kingdom" (NASB, NIV).

Seats (11:16)

The Greek has *thronous,* "thrones" (NASB, NIV).

And Art to Come (11:17)

This clause is not in the ancient Greek text (cf. NASB, NIV).

Testament (11:19)

Diathēkē should be translated "covenant" (NASB, NIV). See discussion at Matt. 26:28 (WM, 1:91).

Wonder (12:1, 3)

The Greek word is *sēmeion,* which means "sign" (NASB, NIV). This is the first vision in Revelation that is called a sign, but we find it again in 13:13. In 15:1 the term is correctly translated "sign" in the KJV. It will be remembered that miracles in the Gospels are called both "wonders" and "signs," but the Greek words are distinct in meaning.

Dragon (12:3)

The Greek word *drakōn* is found (in NT) only in Revelation (13 times; 8 times in this chap.). Foerster notes that *drakōn* had three meanings: "serpent, dragon, and sea-monster" (TDNT, 2:281). It should be remembered that it was "the serpent" who tempted Eve (Gen. 3:14). In Revelation "the dragon" is always Satan. Foerster notes this is "the key image for Satan in the whole book" (p. 282).

In verse 9 the dragon is identified as "that old serpent," called the Devil, and Satan." *Diabolos* ("devil") occurs 38 times in the NT—6 times each in Matthew and Luke, but never in Mark. It is found 5 times in Revelation, and 4 times in 1 John. It means "the slanderer." *Satanas* ("Satan") occurs 36 times in the NT—6 times each in Mark and Luke, and 8 times in Revelation. It means "the adversary." Satan functioned in both capacities, slandering God's people (e.g., Job and v. 10) and opposing God and all His work.

Strength (12:10)

The Greek word is *dynamis,* from which we get *dynamite,* and *dynamo,* and *dynamic.* Rather than "strength" (KJV), it means "power" (NASB, NIV).

The Inhabiters Of (12:12)

These words are not in the Greek (cf. NASB, NIV), though they may be implied.

Persecuted (12:13)

The verb *diōkō* basically means "pursue" and is often used of pursuing good things (Phil. 3:12, 14; Heb. 12:14). But it is used most frequently in a hostile sense, "persecute." Here the dragon (Satan) both "pursued" and "persecuted" the woman.

Flood (12:15, 16)

The Greek word is *potamos,* the regular term for "river" in the NT. In the KJV it is translated "flood" only here and in Matt. 7:25, 27 (where the NIV has "streams").

Cause . . . to Be Carried Away of the Flood (12:15)

All of this is two words in Greek: *potamophorēton poiēsē.* The verb *poieō* means "make." The long word is an adjective (only here in NT), compounded of *potamos,* "river," and the verb *pherō,* "carry." So it means "swept away by a river"—that is, drowned. The dragon was determined to destroy the woman. For the identification of the "woman" here one must consult commentaries.

I Stood (13:1)

Instead of *estathēn,* "I stood" (KJV), which is not found in any Greek manuscript before the ninth century, all the early manuscripts have *estathē,* "he stood." This would be a reference to the dragon, and not to John. It is properly a conclusion to the 12th chapter rather than an introduction to the 13th chapter.

Beast (13:1)

The Greek word is *thērion,* which, as we have seen, means "a wild beast." This beast is what we commonly call "the Antichrist."

Seat (13:2)

The Greek has *thronos,* "throne" (NASB, NIV).

Power (13:4, 5)

The Greek has *exousia,* "authority" (NASB, NIV), not *dynamis,* "power" (KJV).

Forty and Two Months (13:5)

It is obvious that the 42 months, the 1,260 days (12:6), and the "time, and times, and half a time" (12:14) all refer to the same period of three and one-half years. This is the length of "the Great Tribulation"—not seven years, as commonly (and mistakenly) held. This is clear in Revelation and agrees perfectly with Dan. 9:27. It is the second *half* of the 70th "week" (of seven years).

Kindreds . . . Tongues . . . Nations (13:7)

Interestingly, it is here the best Greek text that has the longer reading. It says *pasan phylēn kai laon kai glōssan kai ethnos*—"every tribe, people, language and nation" (NIV; cf. NASB). Incidentally, these are all singular, not plural, in the Greek.

Captivity (13:10)

The word *aichmalōsia* occurs twice in this verse and nowhere else in the NT except Eph. 4:8. It comes from *aichmalōtos* (in NT only in Luke 4:18), "captive," and so means "captivity."

The difference in the wording of this verse in different versions is due largely to the uncertainty as to the exact original text. A dozen variant readings are found in the Greek manuscripts. So we cannot be certain. A. T. Robertson suggests this interpretation for the first part of the verse: "Apparently John means this as a warning to the Christians not to resist force with force, but to accept captivity as he had done as a means of grace" (WP, 6:402).

Miracles (13:14)

The Greek has *sēmeia*, "signs" (NASB, NIV).

Life (13:15)

The Greek has *pneuma*, "breath" (NASB, NIV).

Mark (13:16, 17)

The noun *charagma* comes from the verb *charassō*, "to engrave." So it means a stamp or impress made on an object. Aside from Acts 17:29, the word is found only in Revelation (seven times). It was evidently some kind of an official seal impressed firmly on the right hand or forehead. Imperial seals of that period have been found. It is indicated in verse 17 that the "mark" consisted of the Beast's name or number.

Beasts (14:3)

This should be "living creatures" (see 4:6).

Guile (14:5)

Pseudos means a "falsehood" or a "lie" (NASB, NIV). It is stronger than "guile."

Before the Throne of God (14:5)

These words are not in the best Greek text, which simply has *amōmoi eisin*—"they are blameless."

That Great City (14:8)

The first part of this verse reads in the Greek: *epesen, epesen Babylōn hē megalē*—literally, "It fell, it fell, Babylon the Great" (cf. NASB, NIV).

Wrath (14:8)

Thymos means "passion, hot anger, wrath" (A-S, 210). The NASB has "passion." Rather clearly it means "wrath" in verse 10—"the wrath of God." But that perhaps does not fit here. It may well be that "the maddening wine of her adulteries" (NIV) catches the right thought.

Patience (14:12)

As we have noted several times, *hypomonē* does not mean "patience" (KJV) but "perseverance" (NASB) or "patient endurance" (NIV).

The Son of Man (14:14)

Both the NASB and the NIV have "a son of man." This is because there is no article here in the Greek, as we regularly find with the expression "the Son of Man" in the Gospels. In the Septuagint of Dan. 7:13 we find the same anarthrous construction as here. We also have "like a son of man" (NIV) in Rev. 1:13. And yet everyone agrees that the reference there is to Christ standing in the midst of His Church. So it would seem to be wisest to go along with Swete and with such recent commentators on Revelation as George Ladd and Robert Mounce in saying that in 14:14 we have the Messiah, not an angel.

Marvellous (15:1)

The verbal adjective *thaumastos* (from *thaumazō*, to "marvel" or "wonder at") is found in a quotation from the Septuagint (Matt. 21:42; Mark 12:11), in John 9:30, and 1 Pet. 2:9. It is a strong expression.

Filled Up (15:1)

Here we have the aorist passive indicative of *teleō*, which comes from *telos*, "end." So it means "bring to an end, complete, finish"—hence here "finished" (NASB) or "completed" (NIV). "Filled up" (KJV) would be the verb *pleroō*.

Saints (15:3)

A KJV marginal note says: "or, *nations*, or, *ages*." Actually "saints" *(hagiōn)* has the least support of all three. It is found only in two Greek manuscripts of the 16th century! So it is obviously a late copyist's mistake.

"Nations" *(ethnōn)* is found in A (5th cent.) and P (9th cent.), together with the bulk of the minuscule manuscripts (9th to 15th cent.). "Ages" *(aiōnōn)* is in P[47] (3rd cent.) and Aleph (4th cent.), as well as most of the earliest versions. Personally, we would opt for "King of the ages" (RSV, NIV).

Not (15:4)

In Greek this is the emphatic double negative, *ou mē*— "not by all means." A holy God is to be feared and worshiped.

The Temple of the Tabernacle
of the Testimony (15:5)

This is a very fulsome title for the sacred place. "Temple" is *naos*, "sanctuary." As we have noted before, "tabernacle" is *skēnē*, "tent." And "testimony" is *martyrion*. The reference is rather obviously to "the Tent of the Testimony" (Num. 9:15; 17:7)—that is, the Tabernacle in the Sinai Desert. The sanctuary was the place of God's presence. The word *naos* is also used in verse 6 ("temple").

White (15:6)

The Greek has the adjective *lampros,* which means "bright" (NASB) or "shining" (NIV).

Girded . . . Girdles (15:6)

How much better the NIV: "wore golden sashes around their chests" (cf. 1:13).

Beasts (15:7)

This should be "living creatures" (cf. 4:6).

Vials (15:7)

The Greek word is *phialē* (sing.), which means a shallow "bowl." It occurs (in NT) only in Revelation (12 times). Today "bowls" is better than "vials."

Noisome and Grievous (16:2)

We would not now use these words to describe something painful. The first adjective is *kakos,* which means "bad, evil, harmful, injurious." It may be translated here as "loathsome" (NASB) or "ugly" (NIV).

The second adjective is a stronger one, *ponēros*. It is used in the NT mainly in an ethical sense—"evil" or "wicked." But here it means "painful, serious." It may be translated "malignant" (NASB) or "painful" (NIV).

Sore (16:2, 11)

The noun *helkos* (only here and Luke 16:21) means a "sore" or "ulcer." The corresponding verb *helkoō* is found in Luke 16:20—"covered with sores."

Souls (16:3)

The Greek does have *psychē*. And it is true that it is most commonly translated "soul." But "every living soul" would suggest to most readers "every living human being."

In Kittel's *Theological Dictionary of the New Testament*, vol. 9 (edited by Gerhard Friedrich), Eduard Schweizer treats the term *psychē* with typical German thoroughness (pp. 608-56). He begins by saying:

> At the earliest accessible level, namely, Homer, Greek has no words for our concepts of body and soul. *Sōma* . . . is simply the corpse. . . . *Psychē*, etymologically related to *psychō*, "to blow (to cool)" . . . is . . . the vital force which resides in the members and which comes to expression especially in the breath. . . . This *psychē* leaves man at the moment of death. . . . The soul goes to the underworld. . . . Neither in life nor death does the *psychē* have anything at all to do with the intellectual or spiritual functions of man *(pp. 608-09)*.

After lengthy discussions of the use of *psychē* in classical Greek, Plato and post-Platonists, the OT, and Judaism, Schweizer finally comes to the NT. Here he treats the word as used in the various NT books, finally arriving at Revelation. Then he writes:

> Very much along OT lines is the use of *pasa psychē* . . . in 16:3 except that the added *zōēs* ["living"] empha-

sizes the fact that the reference is to living creatures. . . .
Only here and in 8:9 is *psychē* used for animal life in the
NT; in both cases marine creatures are in view *(p. 653)*.

The Greek literally says: "and every living *psychē* died,
the things [neuter article] in the sea." So it seems that the
best translation is "every living thing in the sea died"
(NASB, NIV). It was a complete destruction.

Lord (16:5)

Instead of "Lord," which would be *kyrios,* the Greek text
has *hosios,* "Holy One" (NASB, NIV). The KJV "Lord"
comes from the Latin Vulgate but has no support in the
Greek manuscripts.

And Shalt Be (16:5)

This clause in the KJV is a late addition made by some
copyist (cf. 11:17). It is not in any good Greek text.

They Are Worthy (16:6)

This sounds like a commendation, which it obviously is
not—quite the opposite! The adjective translated "worthy"
is *axios,* which means "befitting." In the NT it is used mostly
in a good sense. But in a number of passages (in Luke, Acts,
and Romans) it has a bad sense, as here. For this we would
say today: "They deserve it" (NASB; cf. NIV).

Another out of the Altar Say (16:7)

The Greek simply has: "And I heard the altar saying"
(NASB; cf. NIV). The verb *akouō,* "hear," takes the genitive
case (as here) for that from whom or from which the message comes. Here it was "the altar saying," or responding
"yes" (cf. NIV).

Altar (16:7)

The Greek word *thysiastērion* occurs 23 times in the NT (6 in Matthew and 8 in Revelation). It comes from the verb *thysiazō*, to "sacrifice," and so would normally indicate the altar on which sacrifices were offered, outside the sanctuary. This is the usage of the term most of the time (outside of Revelation) in the NT. But in Luke 1:11 it is used for the altar of incense (indicated by the addition of the word for "incense").

Which is it here in Revelation? Abbott-Smith lists it under "the altar of incense in the sanctuary," adding "symbolically in Heaven" for all the passages in Revelation except 11:1, where it is clearly the altar of burnt offering. On the other hand, Westcott writes regarding its first use in Revelation: "The altar of sacrifice: vi.9, which proclaims the justice of God's judgments: xvi.7" (p. 454). Robert Mounce observes: "It is significant that throughout Revelation (except in 11:1) the altar is connected with judgment (6:9; 8:3-5; 9:13; 14:18; 16:7)" (*The Book of Revelation*, 296). As to which altar it is, probably George Ladd gives the best conclusion: "The context does not determine whether the altar is that of incense or of burnt offering; but in either case, the meaning is the same" (p. 211).

Almighty (16:7)

Aside from 2 Cor. 6:18, *pantokratōr* occurs (in NT) only in Revelation (nine times). In the KJV it is translated "Almighty" except in 19:6 ("omnipotent"). The NASB and NIV are consistent in retaining "Almighty" there. The noun comes from *pas*, "all," and the verb *krateō*, "be strong, mighty." Michaelis says that *pantokratōr* means "the almighty," "the ruler of all things" (TDNT, 3:914). He goes on to say: "The reference is not so much to God's activity in creation as to His supremacy over all things" (p. 915).

Devils (16:14)

Daimonion means "demons," not "devils." There is only one devil, but there are many demons. See notes on James 2:19.

Miracles (16:14)

The Greek has *sēmeia*—"signs" (NASB) or "miraculous signs" (NIV).

Of the Earth And (16:14)

These words are not in any good Greek text, but were added later. The Greek simply says "kings of the whole world." The term for "world" here is not *cosmos* but *oikoumenē,* which means "inhabited earth."

Armageddon (16:16)

The Greek word is *Harmagedōn* (only here in NT). This is generally connected with Megiddo, on the border between Samaria and Galilee. *Har* is Hebrew for "mountain."

Talent (16:21)

This would be "about a hundred pounds" (NIV; cf. NASB)—the heaviest hailstones ever to fall from the sky. The Great Tribulation will be a time of the greatest catastrophes ever to befall this earth.

Whore (17:1)

The Greek word is *pornē* (fem.), from which we get *pornography.* Occurring 12 times in the NT, it is translated (KJV) "harlot" 8 times and "whore" 4 times. The masculine term *pornos* occurs 10 times—"fornicator" and "whoremonger" each 5 times. The abstract noun *porneia* is found 26 times and is regularly translated "fornication." As we have noted previously, this is too narrow a meaning; it should be "sexual immorality" (NIV), including fornication and adultery. The same is true of the verb *porneuō* (8 times), rendered "commit fornication."

The proper translation today for *pornē* is "harlot" (NASB) or "prostitute" (NIV). The reference is to "Babylon the great" (14:8; 16:19), a symbolical name for Rome—as almost all commentators agree. The last verse of this chapter seems to prove it.

Committed Fornication . . . Fornication (17:2)

The verb is *porneuō,* the noun *porneia* (see above). The first should be translated "committed acts of immorality" (NASB) or "committed adultery" (NIV). The second means "immorality" (NASB) or "adulteries" (NIV). Swete comments, "The *porneia* of which these kings were guilty consisted in purchasing the favour of Rome by accepting her suzerainty and with it her vices and idolatries" (p. 213).

In the Spirit (17:3)

The Greek is simply *en pneumati* (no article). We find the same phrase in 1:10; 4:2; and 21:10. For the first the KJV has "in the Spirit." But for the other three it has "in the spirit." Both the NASB and NIV have "in the Spirit" in all four places.

Some commentators have interpreted the phrase as meaning "in a trance." Others insist that it is John's "spirit"—"in spirit"—not the Holy Spirit. As we have noted before, the Greek does not have our practice of capital letters at the beginning of some words; so it offers no help at this point. But it does seem best to hold that John was under the influence of the Holy Spirit.

Scarlet Coloured (17:3)

This is one word in Greek, *kokkinos*. The adjective occurs in Matt. 27:28 and Heb. 9:19, but elsewhere only in Revelation (17:3, 4; 18:12, 16). It comes from *kokkos*, which outside the NT was used for the scarlet berry (TDNT, 3:811).

Concerning *kokkinos*, Michel notes, "In the prophets scarlet is often linked with ungodly and sinful conduct" (TDNT, 3:812). He further comments, "Purple and scarlet indicate the worldly pomp of the demonic power *Babylon* in Revelation. The woman sits on a scarlet beast . . . , and she is herself arrayed in purple and scarlet." He then goes on to say:

> Only purple and scarlet fit the deeds of this woman, namely licentiousness, seduction by the wine of unchastity, blasphemies, abominations, and murder of the witnesses of Jesus, 17:1-6. Here red epitomizes demonic abomination, ungodly lasciviousness and the power which is hostile to God *(p. 813)*.

Martyrs (17:6)

The NASB has "witnesses" and the NIV "those who bore testimony." Why the change?

The answer is that the Greek word here, *martyrōn* (gen. pl.), is connected with the verb *martyreō,* which means "to be a witness, bear witness, testify" (A-S, 278). The noun *martys* (nom. sing.) meant "a witness" and was used mainly for a witness in court, though also for any witness. Occurring 34 times in the NT, it is translated "witness" (KJV) 29 times. Only three times is it translated "martyr" (Acts 22:20; Rev. 2:13; 17:6). In Acts 22:20 it is applied to Stephen, the first Christian martyr. This is the only passage in the NT where the NIV uses "martyr." The NASB does not use it at all. Why?

Swete gives the answer. Referring to Acts 22:20 and Rev. 17:6, he writes:

> It is tempting to translate *martys* by 'martyr' in the last two passages, and even R.V. yields to the temptation in Apo.l.c., though it is content to call Stephen and Antipas 'witnesses.' But it may be doubted whether the word had acquired a technical sense ["martyr"] at the end of the first century *(p. 36)*.

Commenting on Rev. 17:6, Strathmann says, "The term *martyres* cannot be taken here in the later martyrological sense" (TDNT, 4:495). So it is perhaps best to avoid using "martyr" in the NT translation. Apparently, this use of *martyr* did not begin until the second century.

Wondered . . . Admiration (17:6)

The Greek has *ethaumasa . . . thauma*. The verb *thaumazō* means to "marvel" or "wonder." The noun *thauma* (only here and 2 Cor. 11:14 in NT) means "wonder." Literally the Greek says, "I wondered a great wonder." So it may be translated "I wondered greatly" (NASB) or "I was greatly astonished" (NIV). There was certainly no "admiration" (KJV) involved!

Marvel (17:7)

This is the same verb, *thaumazo,* as in verse 6.

Perdition (17:8, 11)

The literal meaning of *apōleia* is "destruction" (NASB, NIV).

Power (17:12)

The Greek word is not *dynamis,* "power," but *exousia,* "authority" (NASB, NIV).

Mind (17:13)

The word is *gnōmē.* It occurs again in verse 17, where the KJV translates it "will." The best translation is "purpose" in both places (NASB, NIV).

Power and Strength (17:13)

The Greek has *dynamin kai exousian,* "power and authority" (NASB, NIV).

Lightened (18:1)

Today a person's heavy load may be "lightened." But the verb here, *phōtizō,* means to "light." The earth was "illuminated" (NASB, NIV) by the angel's glory, or splendor.

Mightily with a Strong Voice (18:2)

This is double translation. The Greek simply says: "with a mighty voice" (NASB, NIV)—*en ischyra phōnē.*

Habitation (18:2)

The Greek word is *katoikētērion* (only here and Eph. 2:22 in NT). *Oikos* means "house," and the intensive prefix *kata* suggests really living in the house—so "dwelling place" (NASB) or "home" (NIV). "Babylon the Great" (Rome) had become "a home for demons" (NIV)—not "devils" (KJV).

Hold . . . Cage (18:2)

In both cases it is the same Greek word, *phylakē.* This

first meant "a guard," and then the place where people are
kept under guard, "a prison" (NASB). In Rev. 20:7 Satan,
after a thousand years, is released from "prison" (KJV, RSV,
NASB, NIV). It is the same Greek word as here, *phylakē*.
Bertram writes, "Similarly in Rev. 18:2 the shattered city of
Babylon becomes the kingdom, the final refuge, and also the
place of banishment and the 'prison' of unclean spirits and
the unclean, hated and sinister birds that are outlawed with
them" (TDNT, 9:244).

Hateful (18:2)

Here we have the perfect passive participle *(mem-
isēmenou)* of the verb *miseō,* which means "hate, detest, ab-
hor" (AG, 522). So it would normally mean "hated, detested,
abhorred." But AG prefer for this passage "loathsome" (p.
523). In line with this the NIV has "detestable."

Abundance (18:3)

Strangely, the Greek word is *dynamis,* "power." But
Arndt and Gingrich give, as one meaning, "resource" (p.
208). They note that in Xenophon's *Anabasis* it is used for
"wealth" (NASB).

Delicacies (18:3)

Strēnos (only here in NT) is defined by Abbott-Smith
as "insolent luxury, wantonness" (p. 420). Arndt and Gingrich (p. 771) give "sensuality" (NASB) and "luxury" (cf.
NIV).

Why does the KJV have "delicacies"? In the *Oxford English Dictionary* the first definition of "delicacy" is: "The
quality of being addicted to pleasure or sensuous delights;
voluptuousness, luxuriousness" (3:159). But this is labeled
"obsolete."

Lived Deliciously (18:7, 9)

This is the verb *strēniazō* (only here in NT). It means "lived luxuriously or sensually" (see previous discussion at v. 3).

Judgment (18:9)

The Greek word is *crisis,* which is especially appropriate. This was the crisis of final judgment on "Babylon."

Merchandise (18:11, 12)

The Greek word is *gomos* (in NT only here and Acts 21:3, where the KJV has "burden"). The noun comes from the verb *gemō,* "to be full," which was first used (by Xenophon) for a ship being filled (A-S, 80). So the appropriate translation of *gomos* here is "cargoes" (NASB, NIV).

Thyine (18:12)

This is practically a transliteration of the Greek word here, *thyinos* (only here in NT). It comes from *thyia,* "an African aromatic tree, with ornamentally veined wood of varying colour" (A-S, 209). The Latin name was *citrinus.* So the NASB and NIV have "citron."

Vessels (18:12)

Today "vessel" means a ship. The Greek word here is *skeuos,* which has a great variety of uses. The first meaning given in Arndt and Gingrich is "thing, *object* used for any purpose at all" (p. 754). The most fitting translation here is "articles" (RSV, NIV). The Greek literally says "every article" (NASB).

Ivory (18:12)

The Greek word is the adjective *elephantinos* (only here in NT). This, of course, is because ivory comes from elephant tusks.

Most Precious (18:12)

The Greek has the superlative degree *(timiōtatos)* of the adjective *timios,* which means "costly, highly valued." It is used "primarily of money value" (A-S, 446). So the correct translation is "costly" (NIV) or "very costly" (NASB).

Cinnamon (18:13)

This is almost an exact transliteration of the Greek word *cinnamōmon* (only here in NT).

Odours (18:13)

The Greek word is *thymiama* (in the pl.). It means "incense" (NASB, NIV).

Spice (18:13, NIV)

The Greek word is *amōmon* (only here in NT). The *amomum* (Latin) was "a fragrant plant of India" (A-S, 26). The correct translation is "spice" (RSV, NASB, NIV). This Greek word is missing in the Textus Receptus, and so in the KJV.

Ointments (18:13)

This is *myron,* which occurs 14 times in the NT and is always translated "ointment" in the KJV. A better translation is "perfume" (NASB).

Oil (18:13)

The Greek word *elaion* comes from *elaia,* "an olive tree." Since we use the word *oil* today mostly for petroleum, it is best here to say "olive oil" (NASB, NIV).

Beasts (18:13)

As noted before, we use this term today mainly for wild animals. The Greek word *ktēnos* means a "domesticated animal" (AG, 455). Arndt and Gingrich go on to say: *"Cattle* alone seem to be meant in the combination *ktēnē kai probata* Rv.18:13." (*Probata* is "sheep.")

Chariots (18:13)

The usual word for "chariot" in the NT is *harma* (Acts 8:28, 29, 38; Rev. 9:9). It was a two-wheeled war chariot.

But the Greek word here is *rheda* (only here in NT). It was a four-wheeled vehicle. So perhaps a better translation is "carriage" (NIV).

Slaves (18:13)

The Greek has *sōmatōn* (gen. pl.), "bodies." In his 70-page article on *sōma* in TDNT, Schweizer notes that the word first appears in Homer for a dead "human or animal body" (7:1025). He holds that here in Rev. 18:13 it refers to a "slave" (p. 1058). Adolf Deissmann says categorically: "In Rev. 18:13 *sōmata* stands for slaves" (BS, 160). He notes that the word has this usage in the Septuagint, based on Egyptian custom. Swete calls attention to the fact that "the slave merchant was known as *sōmatemporos"* (p. 234). So "slaves" (KJV, NASB) has considerable support. As for "bodies and souls of men" (NIV), A. T. Robertson makes this suggestion: "Perhaps *kai* ["and"] here should be rendered 'even,' not 'and': 'bodies even souls of men'" (WP, 6:442). It is significant that these come at the very bottom of this list, as least valuable!

Fruits (18:14)

The noun *opōra* (only here in NT) literally meant "late summer, early autumn" (late July through early September). Since that was fruit time, it came to mean "ripe fruits."

Dainty and Goodly (18:14)

The first adjective is *liparos* (only here in NT). It comes from the noun *lipos*, "fat"—that is, rich food. The second adjective is *lampros*, "bright, splendid"—referring here to expensive clothes. So the idea is "luxurious and splendid" (NASB). The NIV ties this in with "all things" (Greek, *panta*) and translates it: "All your riches and splendor."

Wailing (18:15, 19)

The verb *pentheō* means "mourn" and is translated that way (KJV) in 7 out of the 10 times it occurs in the NT. In 2 Cor. 12:21 it is rendered "bewail" and only here (twice) as "wail." So the participle is correctly translated "mourning" (NASB; cf. NIV).

Alas (18:10, 16, 19)

The word *ouai*, doubled here for emphasis, means "alas" (grief) or "woe" (denunciation) in NASB, NIV.

Decked (18:16)

We have here the perfect passive participle of the verb *chrysoō* (only here and 17:4). It comes from *chrysos*, "gold," and so means "gilded" or "covered with gold." In both these passages it is followed by the noun for gold (*chrysion,* diminutive of *chrysos,* and so meaning gold ornament). The combination may be translated "adorned with gold" (NASB) or "glittering with gold" (NIV).

Shipmaster (18:17)

Kybernētēs is found (in NT) only here and Acts 27:11 (see discussion there, WM, 2:164). It primarily means "pilot" but may also be translated "sea captain" (NIV).

Costliness (18:19)

The noun is *timiotēs* (only here in NT). It obviously comes from *timē,* "honor." But all lexicons agree that it means "costliness" or "wealth" (NASB, NIV).

Holy Apostles and Prophets (18:20)

The Greek reads: *hoi hagioi kai hoi apostoloi kai hoi prophētai. Hoi* is the definite article (nom. pl. masc.). *Kai* is "and." *Hagioi* is the nominative plural masculine of the adjective *hagios,* "holy." In the NT this adjective is often used as a substantive: "holy ones" or "saints." The structure here clearly shows that the correct translation is "saints and apostles and prophets" (RSV, NASB, NIV).

Harpers (18:22)

Kitharōdon (only here and 14:2 in NT) comes from *kithara,* "harp" (1 Cor. 14:7; Rev. 5:8; 14:2; 15:2). Today we would call these players "harpists" (NASB, NIV).

Pipers (18:22)

Aulētēs (sing.) is found only here and Matt. 9:23 in NT.

It comes from the verb *auleō,* "play on a flute." In the genitive plural here *(aulētōn)* it means "flute players" (NIV).

Craftsman . . . Craft (18:22)

The former is *technitēs* (only here and Acts 19:24, 38; Heb. 11:10). The latter is *technē* (only here and Acts 17:29; 18:3). We get *technician* from *technitēs.*

Candle (18:23)

This, of course, is "lamp." They had no candles in those days.

Sorceries (18:23)

The Greek word is *pharmakeia,* from which we get *pharmacy.* See discussion at 9:21.

Honour (19:1)

This is not found in the early Greek manuscripts. It is obviously a later addition, not a part of the inspired text.

Beasts (19:4)

This should be "living creatures." See discussion at 4:6.

Omnipotent (19:6)

This is *pantokratōr.* The better translation is "Almighty" (NASB, NIV). See discussion at 16:7.

Honour (19:7)

The Greek word is *doxa,* "glory" (NASB, NIV).

Marriage (19:7, 9)

Gamos is better translated "wedding" (NIV). In John 2:1-3 it obviously refers to the wedding festivities more than to the marriage itself. Abbott-Smith defines the word as meaning *"a wedding,* esp. *a wedding-feast"* (p. 88).

Opened (19:11)

This is the perfect passive participle of *anoigō,* "open." So it means "standing open" (NIV). See discussion at 4:1.

Crowns (19:12)

Eight times in the Book of Revelation (2:10; 3:11; 4:4, 10; 6:2; 9:7; 12:1; 14:14) we have had the word *stephanos,* which means "a victor's crown." It occurs 10 times in the rest of the NT.

But here we have a different term, *diadēma,* which means "a royal crown." In the NT it is found only 3 times, all in Revelation (12:3; 13:1; 19:12). That is why the NASB has here "diadems" (which we get from *diadēma*). Christ is pictured in Revelation as wearing both kinds of crowns.

Fowls (19:17, 21)

Today we use the term "fowls" mainly for chickens. The *Am. Heritage Dict.* (p. 520) says that the use of "fowl" for "any bird" is "archaic." The Greek term here, *orneios* (pl.) means "birds" (NASB, NIV). The word is found (in NT) only here and 18:2.

The Supper of the Great God (19:17)

The RSV, NASB, and NIV all have "the great supper of God." Why the difference? The answer is that the Greek says: *to deipnon to mega tou theou.* Obviously *mega,* "great," goes with *deipnon,* "supper," and not with *theou,* which is in the genitive case ("of God").

Captains (19:18)

The Greek word is *chiliarchos,* an officer in charge of a thousand men—which is something more than a captain. The correct translation is "commanders" (NASB) or "generals" (NIV). See discussion at 6:15.

Bottomless Pit (20:1, 2)

See discussion at 9:1.

Lived (20:4)

The Greek has the aorist tense, *ezēsan.* This may well be the ingressive aorist: "came to life" (NASB, NIV). The same form is found in verse 5: "did not come to life" (NASB, NIV).

From God (20:9)

This phrase is not in the text of any manuscript earlier than the ninth century, and so is omitted in all scholarly versions today.

Before God (20:12)

The early Greek manuscripts all have "before the throne" *(thronos),* not "God" *(theos).* See the RSV, NASB, and NIV.

Hell (20:13, 14)

The Greek word is *hadēs,* which should be transliterated "Hades" (all good versions). As we have noted before, *hadēs* was the place of departed spirits. "Hell," the place of eternal punishment, is clearly designated here as "the lake of fire" (vv. 14-15). The fact that it says that *hadēs* was "cast into the lake of fire" (v. 14) clearly shows that *hadēs* does not mean hell. It should always be called Hades.

John (21:2)

Lest anyone wonder why this word (KJV) is not in the recent versions, we would simply note that it is not in the Greek.

Adorned (21:2)

This is the verb *cosmeō,* in the perfect passive participle, *kecosmēmenēn.* As we have noted before, *cosmeō* (from which we get *cosmetics*) means to "order, arrange, adorn." The NIV has here: "beautifully dressed."

Heaven (21:3)

The Greek says *tou thronou,* "the throne" (RSV, NASB, NIV). Some late copyist substituted *ouranou,* "heaven," probably from verse 2, and this got in the Textus Receptus.

Freely (21:6)

This might be interpreted as meaning abundantly. But the Greek word *dōrea* comes from the verb *didōmi,* "give," and so means "a gift." Here the accusative case, *dōrean,* is used adverbially in the sense of "gratis, without payment," or "without cost" (NASB, NIV).

Fearful (21:8)

The adjective *deilos* means "fearful," or "cowardly" (NASB, NIV).

Abominable (21:8)

This is the perfect passive participle of *bdelyssō* (only here and Rom. 2:22), which comes from *bdeō*, "stink." So it means "abominable," or "vile" (NIV).

Whoremongers (21:8)

As we have noted before, *pornē* (fem., found in 17:1, 5, 15, 16; 19:2) and the word here (and 22:15), *pornos* (masc.), in the plural meant "immoral persons" (NASB) or "the sexually immoral" (NIV). Immorality was very common in the Roman Empire of the 1st century, and it is rampant in the 20th century!

The Second Death (21:8)

The first death is physical and temporary. The second death is spiritual and eternal. It has well been said: "Born twice, die once; born once, die twice."

In the Spirit (21:10)

See discussion at 4:2.

That Great City, the Holy Jerusalem (21:10)

The Greek has: *tēn polin tēn hagian Ierousalēm.* This clearly says: "the holy city, Jerusalem" (NASB; cf. NIV).

Light (21:11)

Phōstēr (only here and Phil. 2:15) means "light-giving body," and so here "splendor, radiance" (AG, 872). A good translation is "brilliance" (NASB, NIV).

Furlongs (21:16)

The Greek says "12,000 *stadia*" (NIV). A *stadion* was the basic measurement for running in the Greek races, about 600 feet. We have taken over into English the Latin form, *stadium,* for a place where races and other athletic events take place. Here the NASB gives the English equivalent of 12,000 stadia: "fifteen hundred miles." (The NIV often gives the English equivalent for weights and measures, but does not do so here.)

An Hundred and Forty and Four Cubits (21:17)

The Greek word *pēchys* (Matt. 6:27; Luke 12:25; John 21:8; Rev. 21:17) is used by Homer for "the forearm." Then it came to be used for "a cubit," the principal unit of measurement of length in the Bible. The Egyptians started using the length of the forearm for a standard of measure (about 18 inches), and it was naturally taken over by the Jews for the measurements of the ancient Tabernacle. Here, again, the NASB has the modern English equivalent, "seventy-two yards," while the NIV has "144 cubits" (a literal translation).

Building (21:18)

The Greek word is *endōmēsis* (only here in NT). It comes from the verb *dōmaō,* "build," and so means "a building in." Abbott-Smith would translate the passage here: "its wall had jasper built into it" (p. 153). Swete suggests the meaning as: "the wall had *iaspis* built into it, it was cased with precious stone, so that it sparkled with crystalline radiance" (p. 290).

Garnished (21:19)

This again is the perfect passive participle of the

verb *cosmeō* (see discussion at v. 2). Here it is translated "adorned" (NASB) and "decorated" (NIV).

Sardius (21:20)

The Greek word is *sardion* (only here and 4:3; see discussion there). The NIV translates it "carnelian."

Chrysoprasus (21:20)

The Greek term *chrysoprasos* (only here in NT) comes from *chrysos,* "gold." Swete says that it "was akin to the beryl, but of a paler green" (p. 293). The King James translators were greatly influenced by the Vulgate, and so they give the Latin form here. The RSV, NASB, and NIV have the modern English form, "chrysoprase."

Lighten (21:23)

See discussion at 18:1.

Light (21:23)

The Greek word is *lychnos,* "lamp" (RSV, NASB, NIV).

Of Them Which Are Saved (21:24)

These words are not in the Greek text and so are omitted in most versions.

And Honour (21:24)

This is not found in the early Greek manuscripts and so should be omitted. It was imported here from verse 26 by some late copyist.

That Defileth (21:27)

This is the Greek adjective *koinos,* which literally means "common" (Acts 2:44; 4:32; Titus 1:4; Jude 3). But in the Septuagint and the NT it is normally used in the sense of "unhallowed" or "unclean" (Matt. 7:2, 5; Acts 10:14, 28; 11:8; Rom. 14:14; Heb. 10:29; and here). So the proper translation is "unclean" (NASB) or "impure" (NIV).

In the Midst of the Street of It (22:2)

Should this start a new sentence for verse 2 (KJV), or should it be attached to verse 1, completing the sentence there (RSV, NASB, NIV)? Probably this question is not important enough for us to be "hung up" on it. The essential thing is to get the spiritual truth so vividly portrayed here: "the river of the water of life" and "the tree of life" forming the central focus of the city, guaranteeing eternal life to all who live there. We should perhaps remind ourselves again that the Greek manuscripts have no verse divisions and no punctuation marks. So they do not help us answer our question here.

Candle (22:5)

The correct translation is "lamp."

The Lord God of the Holy Prophets (22:6)

The Greek reads: *ho kyrios ho theos tōn pneumatōn tōn prophētōn* —"the Lord, the God of the spirits of the prophets" (RSV, NASB, NIV).

Saw . . . Heard (22:8)

The Greek has: *Kagō Iōannēs ho akouōn kai blepōn tauta* —literally, "and I John, the one hearing and seeing these things." *(Kagō is for kai egō.)* The best translation is: "and I, John, am the one who heard and saw these things" (NASB; cf. NIV)—an emphatic statement.

He That Is Unjust . . . (22:11)

The Greek literally reads: "The one doing wrong, let him still do wrong; and the filthy one, let him still be filthy [verb only here in NT]; and the righteous one, let him still do righteousness; and the holy one, let him still be holy."

The Beginning . . . the First . . . (22:13)

These clauses are the reverse of the Greek text (cf. NASB, NIV).

They That Do His Commandments (22:14)

This represents the Greek: *poiountes tas entolas autou.* But that is not found in any manuscript earlier than the 10th century. The 4th- and 5th-century manuscripts, with several later ones, have: *plynontes tas stolas autōn*—"who wash their robes" (NASB, NIV).

The Bright and Morning Star (22:16)

There is no *kai* in the Greek between the two adjectives. They go together: "the bright Morning Star" (NIV; cf. NASB). The adjective "Morning" is *prōinos* (only here and 2:28). It means "at early morn."

Come . . . Come . . . Come . . . (22:17)

All too often we hear this verse read in public as if all three occurrences of "come" were parallel. The readers have given them equal emphasis. But the first two are quotations

("Come!") while the third is indirect and should be sounded differently. This is helped by the wording in the NIV.

You All (22:21)

The NASB has just "all," while the NIV has "God's people." Why these differences?

Again we have a textual problem. Manuscript A (5th cent.) has *pantōn,* "all." Aleph (4th cent.) has *tōn hagiōn,* "the saints" or "God's people." Only one extremely late manuscript (16th cent.) has "you all." We cannot be certain what the original text was. But, as we have said before, the essential meaning of the passage is not affected adversely by these variant readings.